FORK AND SPOON DIARY

BY

GIBRAN TARIQ

ACKNOWLEDGEMENTS

Gibran Tariq
I acknowledge that the children are our future.

(Aaliyah Mahogany Black)
1/7/2010

BOOK 1

CHAPTER ONE

This was not a good beginning.

The second most memorable thing of the new day was that church was going to start in a few hours. The first was the argument Trina Brown and her mother were having.

"Sweetheart," Alfreda, a pretty, dark-skinned woman in her forties, flatly stated, "you are not going to compete in the Miss Teen Charlotte beauty pageant so you just as well get used to the idea."

"But, Mama," Trina protested, "I am pretty enough to win." Spinning her 5'2" chocolate frame around on her toes, she chanted. "I have classic beauty....just like you."

"Young lady-----"

"I'll be miserable if I don't participate," Trina interrupted softly.

"*Miserable?*" Alfreda commented wisely. "Not hardly. Misery is too grown up. Honey, you are only seventeen."

"Still, I want to compete."

Alfreda shook her head. "The world needs leaders, not beauty queens. I'm sure your father would tell you the same thing."

"Mama, why did you have to mention daddy when you know that all he believes the world needs is more boxing champions?" Trina smiled. "You know you can hardly talk to him about anything without him talking about how the universe needs someone to fill the boxing gloves of Muhammad Ali."

That's not fair to your father," Alfreda snapped. "Boxing is the only thing he knows."

Trina pouted. "A boxer always gets another chance to regain his title, but, for a woman, sometimes there is only one chance to do what her heart tells her to do."

"Well, you're not a woman yet." Alfreda shrugged her shoulders wearily. "Maybe young girls get second chances."

"Not so quick, Mama----"

Alfreda stopped her daughter in mid-sentence. "Don't you think you need to get ready for church?"

At the mention of church, the vibrant excitement Trina had felt earlier jumped to life again and she found it hard to breathe or to think clearly. She clasped her hands across her chest, hoping to slow down her heart which beat under her Sunday school dress like an African drum. She prayed the special guest would show up.

She had learned long ago not to defy her parents, but in her head where she kept all her secrets, she could clearly see herself competing and winning the title of Miss Teen Charlotte. And after that, Miss Teen USA. No one could dispute her beauty. She was as dark as the finest African cocoa bean and her ebony skin was flawless and clear.

Any time anyone from the small community where she lived in Charlotte zeroed in on her very distinct facial features, the one thing they all agreed upon was that she had been blessed with all the chromosomes of a beauty queen. Yet despite all this mental evidence, Trina hid what she felt in her heart because she didn't want to encourage herself to believe in something her parents were against. She continued dressing.

But sometimes, Trina would not, as some of the older folk said, leave well enough alone.

"Please forgive me, Mama," Trina said softly, "but doesn't beauty count for anything any more?"

Alfreda smiled slyly. "Sometimes, it does and sometimes it doesn't." When she saw the confused look on her daughter's face, Alfreda patted Trina's shoulder tenderly. "The strange thing about beauty," she lectured, "is that it is two-faced. It can be a curse as

3

much as it can be a blessing, and without wisdom to understand the difference, it can lead to trouble."

"But I am smart," Trina said.

That remark made Trina's father, Ken, a short, hard-working businessman, who had just walked into the room, laugh and when he saw that his daughter was about to speak, he put his finger to his lips to quiet her. He coughed, clearing his throat. "Always remember and never forget that beauty without brains is like a fine car without an engine. It looks wonderful, but where can it take you?" He grinned. "This country does not need pretty faces, it needs strong minds"

When Trina couldn't drum up a good enough reason to debate with her strong-willed father, she sighed. "I am ready for church now." However, that didn't mean she was giving up on the idea that she was the picture perfect candidate to represent the state of North Carolina in the upcoming Miss Teen USA beauty pageant.

She smiled. Sometimes parents just didn't understand.

On her way to church with her family, Trina didn't have any problems believing that today was going to be special. She pondered that notion, agreed with it, and then settled back to see what would happen next. Then something else occurred to her. Today was not just going to be special, it was going to be spectacular. And just in case, God hadn't noticed her first smile of appreciation for what was about to happen in her young life, she flashed a second one. This time, the smile stretched across her face from ear to ear, tickling her nose and turning her lips up like an upside-down half-moon.

The church, though a somber grey on the outside, was bright and spacious inside. It was also spotless. Sinking back into one of the pews as close to the front as she and her family could get, Trina savored the possibilities of finding clues and signs today to make her parents rethink their position about the beauty contest, but when she spotted Shonda Grier, seated across the aisle from her, she groaned. The expression on Shonda's face was identical to hers. Shonda was already a contest entrant so Trina guessed that now the girl was in church to search for clues and signs that would answer her prayers to win the title of Miss Teen Charlotte.

Shonda smiled.

Trina smiled back.

It was the same smiles they treated each other to just before they took a test, the thrill of anticipation to see who would get the highest grade. Shonda had outscored her on the last two exams by only a few points, but like in sports, a loss was a loss no matter if you lost by one point or a hundred.

"Don't pay her any mind," Trina told herself.

Meanwhile, in the pulpit, Reverend Ebenezer's voice boomed. "It was my hopes to secure the honorable presence of the woman we all know and love as The First Lady of the United States but after her appearance at the CIAA tournament, she had other business to attend to. As we should all be aware, Mrs. Obama has been busy lobbying in this country to get the nation to adopt a more healthy approach to eating." Reverend Ebenezer stared down lovingly at his congregation. "Let no one here today be discouraged or disappointed that The First Lady cannot be here because she is doing her part to uplift the country out of its dietary graveyard, but can she do it alone? Should she do it alone? No, because it is the duty of all Americans to help in this mighty cause."

Trina listened in rapt attention as the reverend spoke of the need of all Americans to use food festivals, such as A Taste of Charlotte not as a reason to merely celebrate, but also to feed the poor and to purify their communities with offerings of peace and goodwill. A tingle ran up her spine.

Reaching into his jacket pocket, Reverend Ebenezer removed a white handkerchief and wiped his sweaty brow. After a brief pause, he resumed his sermon.

"I would like to take this time," he thundered, "to publicly announce an event that can only be termed historic so I invite you to listen carefully." Reverend Ebenezer grinned, and soon a full smile tickled his mustache, accenting his round face. "A new organization, The Eating Well Chamber of Commerce has kicked off its first annual "Pilgrimage to Wellness" project. This project was established to assist African-Americans who want to visit the land of good health." The reverend grinned even more. "The opportunity is now yours so don't ever let anyone tell you that you can't get to the Garden of Eden. Suddenly, you can get there from here."

Caught up now in the rapture of good eating and healthy living, Trina was enchanted as Reverend

Ebenezer rolled off a list of places where the tour to wellness would stop. She leaned forward to listen more closely, getting more and more excited as she heard that the tour would touch down in places such as the Castle of Fruits and Vegetables, the Whole Grain Centre, The Pond of Natural Drink as well as the infamous Processed Food Mausoleum. And as if these were not enough, the tourists would also get a chance to witness other great gastronomic venues.

Trina smiled at the colorful imagery of the mythical, mystical journey and for a brief moment in time, forgot about becoming Miss Teen Charlotte.

Reverend Ebenezer turned serious. He pushed his tall body upright until he was almost rigid. "How hypocritical is it of parents who don't think twice about taking their child the long way home to simply avoid the guy on the street corner who is selling drugs, but don't hesitate to take that same beloved child into the corner grocery store and then buy that child a soft drink loaded with chemicals more dangerous than any found in drugs." Reverend Ebenezer paused to take a deep breath. "I pity the parent who has not yet realized that the fork and spoon are deadlier than the crack pipe! But there is something else you need to know. Eating has become one of our biggest disappointments, and we have become so naturally good at eating that we are killing ourselves. We are the foolish prisoners of our palettes. We listen to our tongues. We invest such culinary stock in what great pleasure we derive from our tongues that we pay scant heed to the potential damage that could be wreaked on our bodies. We are such suckers for our tongues that we suffer proudly when our tummies ache due to some gastronomical violation."

Trina believed.

CHAPTER TWO

The Pilgrimage to Wellness was an event that didn't unfold slowly. It exploded, thundering into a vast experience of vivid color and motion. Trina had never seen so much food.

The first thing she had done that Saturday morning had been to attend a parade where many of the participants had pranced down McDowell Street dressed as brightly-colored vegetables and sun-kissed fruits. Then, after the parade she had bounced merrily from booth to booth where she had tasted organic and vegan foods from all over the world. She never knew that such delicious dishes existed and though some of these exotic foods did seem foreign to her the first time she had sampled them, she took this as a sign that she had lost contact with her true food roots. Her palette, as Reverend Ebenezer had preached, had been bamboozled.

In an all-out drive not to miss anything, Trina loved the joy of being caught up in the national pastime of getting healthy. She bought a flag with the food pyramid emblazoned on it. Next, she donated a dollar to a fund to fight childhood obesity. And another to help in the battle to find a cure for juvenile diabetes Then, she dashed over to the concert stage where superstars, Erykah Badu, and Earth, Wind, and Fire would perform. She was also eager to watch the Ghana Dance Ensemble.

By the time the concert was finished, Trina was all fire and brimstone, and within seconds found herself standing in the middle of a political rally. Even though she was more of a spiritual person than a political one, she persuaded herself to stay and to listen to the speakers who lined the stage, praising the wonder of natural living and eating. She was instantly drawn into the drama, fascinated by the speakers' bold predictions and warnings. The electricity here crackled with more intensity than at the concert. She pushed closer to the stage.

On the platform, a dark-skinned African exchange student who attended Johnson C. Smith University talked loudly, speaking out against the nutritionally-deficient cafeteria food served in high schools in the United States. Trina had never heard such a speech.

"This," the speaker said, "will not be the land of the healthy when the food served in jail is more nutritious than the food served up in lunch rooms in schools across this country." When the man spoke next, he stared directly at Trina. "Which is better," he barked harshly, "to be a wealthy, beauty queen or the queen of a beautiful, healthy life?"

Stumbling away from the platform in a daze, Trina carried a mixed bag of emotions inside her head. Everything seemed odd and for some reason, she now felt guilty. It was almost as if the man had somehow accused her of treason. Suddenly, she needed to retreat so she could fix things in her mind, but after a bitter, internal argument with herself, she still wanted to compete in the beauty pageant.

Ten minutes later as Trina weaved her way carefully through the throng of people in their colorful garb, she turned left at the concession stand where fried plantains were being prepared. She intentionally by-passed her destination, stopped at the booth next to it, admired some crafts, and after buying a strip of kente cloth was ready to stand in front of the huge stage where a fashion and beauty show was being presented. Trina gasped at the sheer beauty of the young girls onstage. The models, from all over the city, were stunning. Many of these women, she knew, would compete for the title of Miss Teen Charlotte.

Without warning, a loud burst of laughter erupted next to her. "I knew I would find you here." It was the young university student who had spoke at the rally a few minutes ago.

Startled, Trina grew angry. "I beg your pardon."

"I knew you would turn up here."

"Are you following me?" Trina snapped.

"The student studied Trina. "The question you need ask yourself is this: Are you worthy of being followed?" The student grinned. "With so much at stake, I think that is a fair question." He extended his hand. "My name is Kofi."

Trina folded her arms defiantly across her chest. "How may I help you?"

Kofi's smile widened as he eyed the stage. "You think that being a beauty queen is the best thing you can do with your life, don't you?"

Trina stood stiffly, surprised that a total stranger knew so much about her. "What I do is none of your business."

"Whether you believe it or not, your welfare is my business." Kofi looked Trina up and down boldly. "When I look at you, I see much more than great beauty. I also see great courage and strength."

"Well, maybe you need to stop looking. Has that ever crossed your mind?" Trina cracked.

"Okay, okay," Kofi conceded, "I don't want to argue with you, Miss Dark and Lovely."

"My name is Trina."

"Tell me something, Trina. Do you believe that everything happens for a reason?"

Trina was getting angrier. "I don't know what kind of game you think you are playing, but I will tell you that I'm not the one. Not only that, but I'm not interested in anything else you have to say. Go play your silly, little game with some other girl. I don't have the time."

Kofi threw up his hands in apparent defeat. "You win, my sister, but I assure you that this is no game. I have no scheme." He thrust a pamphlet into Trina's hands. "Here, read this, 'The Fork and Spoon Chronicles'. "You might find something that may interest you." When he saw Trina gaze at the pamphlet curiously, Kofi lowered his voice. "I know that you believe that you came here for this," he said, casting a glance at the models on the stage, "but sometimes you get more than you bargained for." He leaned closer. "There is an old wise African proverb that proclaims that when you pick up one end of a stick, you also pick up the other end of the stick."

Kofi disappeared into the crowd.

Later that evening as she studied the pamphlet for a third time, it seemed natural enough that the gang of words would lose some of their original sting. They didn't, so she shuffled through the documents once more. Just to be on the safe side, she turned on the lamp beside her bed to shed some light on the paper.

They---*whoever they were*---wanted her to join them!

Later this year, according to the documents, Kofi and his friends were starting The Healthy Student Coalition. And that was just for starters. Trina closed her eyes tightly, then opened them slowly. She thought about the aims of the HSC which was to unify mind and body and to introduce holistic health practices into American public schools.

According to The Fork and Spoon Chronicles, most high school students had unhealthy cholesterol levels which would follow them into adulthood. Trina also learned that just as soon as most teenagers became more independent, they became less dependent on eating at home. This was also a time when teens became stressed with body image and obsessed with keeping up with their peers that they used food as a coping mechanism, and it was this emotional eating that got them into trouble.

Studies have shown that sugary soft drinks, the kind most favored by teens, have little nutritional value but contains a lot of phosphoric acid which decreases bone growth.

Trina shuddered in disgust as she discovered that most processed bread contained L-cysteine which was made from dissolved human hair. Food corporations added the substance to the dough as conditioner to improve the texture of the bread.

Next she found that titanium dioxide, an ingredient used in paint which is contaminated with toxic lead was added to salad dressing to make them appear whiter.

By the time she read that canned mushrooms had maggots, she was ready to vomit.

For a lot of reasons, Trina still didn't want to get involved.

But there were many reasons why she should.

Bothered by her choice to hide everything from her parents, Trina decided she needed to take a walk. Maybe it would refresh her. Walking down the street, she did wonder about the so-called "enlightened brotherhood and sisterhood" of those who would lead the HSC. Though, she had been given no precise figures, it was clear that a lot of the university students would be involved. She wondered where a seventeen year old high school student like her would fit in.

Careful to look both ways before crossing a busy intersection on Central Avenue, Trina was only mildly annoyed when she reached the other side of the street and found Kofi standing there, grinning widely.

"Don't worry. I am not a stalker and you can't say that I'm following you because I was here first."

"But why are you here or do you like hanging out at bus stops? If so, maybe you should mention it in your next edition of HSC news."

"So you have been reading the material." Kofi seemed to enjoy that notion. "What do you think?" Failing to wring an answer from Trina with his eyes, he pretended that it didn't matter, but after a second his curiosity got the best of him. "Well?"

Trina sighed. "Of course, I'm interested. Who doesn't want to be healthy?"

"Then, as a concerned student, you must join us."

"No, I don't, either," Trina snapped. She began to walk down the street. "No one can make me do anything I don't want to do." She pointed a finger at Kofi. "Especially you."

"You're so pretty when you're mad."

"I thought this was about health?" Trina cracked coldly. "Or is there something else on your mind that I need to set you straight about?"

Kofi dropped his head. "I'm sorry. I couldn't help myself, but you must know how beautiful you are."

"If it's just the same to you," Trina scolded, "I'd like to be seen as smart."

"Then why would you want to participate in a beauty contest?" Kofi eyes twinkled mischievously. "Gotcha."

"So I could help people, that's why?" Trina was fuming.

Kofi stopped walking. "Are you crazy? No one in their right minds will take you seriously once you----"

"Evidently, you haven't heard of Gifty Adu-Darko, the beauty queen from Ghana, who produced and directed the hit movie 'Here Comes the Boom'."

"Yes, I know of her and her work. I applaud it, but young people need a lot more than entertainment. They need enlightenment."

"Like what?" Trina was ready to argue.

"Like everything."

"Nice try." Trina started back down the street, then turned abruptly. "I think I better be going home now. You can't reform people."

"Not reform them," Kofi corrected, "but save them. We must save Americans, especially black Americans from obesity, from diabetes, from hypertension; from an early grave." Pausing to let the info sink in, Kofi continued. "You just said a minute ago that you wanted to help our people. Well, the time is now."

CHAPTER THREE

"How can anyone explain stupidity?"

Across the table, Trina smiled weakly. She offered a slight shrug. "Ugh".

"Who introduced you to the HSC?"

Trina made a face, but said nothing.

Reverend Ebenezer smiled. "My goodness, you wouldn't be the first girl in the history of the world, especially at the tender age of seventeen, to fall for the glory of helping our people." The reverend winked knowingly. "Plus, it's fairly easy to get caught up in the mix, as you young ones say, when the boys with the invitation are cute."

Trina looked away.

"Come on now, my friend," Reverend Ebenezer replied calmly, "who says that trouble can't come in pretty packages." With that, he got up from the kitchen table, went to the refrigerator, and soon returned with two small bowls of chocolate ice cream. "I'm not trying to bribe you." He pushed one of the bowls towards Trina. "Enjoy."

"Thanks."

"Say what you like," Reverend Ebenezer said, "but I am not opposed to any group that really works to help our cause, but I wouldn't want you to get caught up in the whirlwind where all you end up with is a heartache."

He watched Trina for a reaction before going on. His voice was filled with despair. "Sometimes, young girls, such as yourself, end up celebrating at the wrong end of the stick."

"And what is that supposed to mean?" Trina got up and carried her empty bowl to the sink. "As a little girl, I was taught that love is good."

"And, trust me, it is, but it would be a fantasy to believe in knights in shining armor. Neither heroes nor husbands just ride up out of nowhere to sweep young damsels in distress off their feet and then carry them into a world where there are happy endings."

Trina could only laugh. "This is not about love. It's about doing my part."

"And I believe you. I really do, but I also believe that right now you may be more attracted to the messenger than the message." Reverend Ebenezer's tone became fatherly. "It's called the cult of personality and when you get right down to it, it is a hard habit to break." He sighed. "It's dangerous. I know because I speak from personal experience."

Trina looked at the reverend, surprised.

"That's right, my young friend, I know all about it." Feeling self-conscious, Reverend Ebenezer whispered. "Women get this notion that I am powerful or smart or something else silly and they start to focus on me instead of my message. Do you understand what I'm trying to say?"

Trina understood.

"Just promise me this," Reverend Ebenezer announced somberly, "that whatever you do, you will at least look before you leap."

"I will," Trina promised. "I'm glad I came to talk to you."

"And so am I." Once Reverend Ebenezer had escorted Trina to the front door of his home, he rubbed his chin thoughtfully. "Can you come by again tomorrow? I'd like for you to have a word with my wife." When he saw a look of alarm cross Trina's face, he quickly added. "She will not say a word about any of this to your parents. No matter what you decide to do, it is your duty to inform your parents of what you intend to do with your life. We—my wife and I—are only here to make sure you are comfortable with the stick you pick up because it's impossible, as you have already been told, to pick up one end of a stick without picking up the other end."

Sitting in her room later that same day, Trina wondered how her parents would react if they if they learned what she was up to. Would they be surprised or shocked? Perhaps they would be amazed and stunned. Either way, today would mark the first day of her new beginning. She was going to become a health food activist.

She sat cross-legged in the middle of her bed, trying hard to remember where she had read that life was nothing more than a wild goose chase without some adventure tossed in as an exclamation point! So far, there had been no exclamation points in her young life. Trina giggled. Her life had been a story filled with commas and periods where she had been told to either slow down or to stop. *No exclamation points!* She wondered how many of her peers felt like they had been edited out of their own lives, or that their parents used their teenage years to punish them. Maybe the years between thirteen and nineteen were the *"payback years"* where parents secretly got revenge on their children for keeping them awake at night when they were babies, for crying in the middle of a favorite show, or for having to be changed while dinner was on the stove.

Trina smiled. Her next English paper might be entitled: *The Secret Vendetta of Mom and Dad.*

She quickly stopped smiling when she found herself fumbling with a reason not to think of Kofi. She couldn't ignore her thoughts of him nor did she wish too. Trina sighed. It was almost as if she was becoming a pawn in a game where her head and her heart were in a custody battle for her soul. This tormented her because she didn't want to end up as a victim of either a hard head or a foolish heart. But Kofi was cute. And charismatic.

Trina shifted her weight on the bed uncomfortably, and just as she was momentarily unable to decide what to do next, she remembered the phone number scribbled across the bottom of the end sheet of the HSC papers. She wondered if the number belonged to Kofi.

She dialed the number.

Once she had finished her call, she attended to the few household chores her mother had assigned her such as making sure her room was clean and taking out the trash. She then dashed out of the house to catch the bus uptown. As luck would have it, The HSC was having a meeting in the main Library in Center City.

The trip took thirty minutes and as soon as she stepped foot inside the conference room, she saw him. Trina hurriedly took a seat, but even from across the crowded room, she could see how good-looking Kofi was. She wanted to get closer to where he stood, talking rapidly to a small group of young ladies who seemed more like admirers than supporters.

From this safe distance, she studied Kofi, who had on a tank top, and Trina couldn't help but notice that he was constructed like a dark, chocolate tank. Real sturdy. Even his long dreads with their carefully-dyed tips looked healthy and muscular.

When Kofi turned himself slightly to the left to get introduced to yet another young lady, he glanced in her direction. He waved when he saw her. That shocked Trina. *A wave!* She had expected—had prayed for and had wanted---so much more than that. *A wave!* Maybe Reverend Ebenezer had been right. Maybe she was trying to pick up the wrong end of the stick.

Trina was amazed at how fast she left the room.

Just as quickly, Kofi was at her side.

"I don't remember sending for you," Trina snapped angrily, "so why don't you go right on back where you came from or do I have to show you how to get there?"

Kofi shook his head. "What did I do?"

"What do you want?"

Kofi chuckled, "You're still the prettiest girl I have ever seen in my life, but you sure don't seem like the same sweet person you were the last time we saw each other." Wondering how it had come to this, he felt driven to say something, to do something that would improve his chances of making Trina smile. "Those other girls don't mean anything to me."

"Could have fooled me."

After urging Trina to calm down, Kofi repeated his message. "Those girls don't mean anything to me." He paused. "You do."

Instantly, Trina felt her anger receding as she was dragged under by the powerful weight of her feelings. "What was the meeting about?"

"Wanna go back and see?"

"No, you tell me while you walk me to the bus stop.""

After a slow start, Kofi filled Trina in on the fact that since the HSC was just starting, they were in search of a leader. "Do you want the job?" he teased.

"Seems like you got the position wrapped up," Trina shot back.

"How about if I told you, I didn't want it."

"What?!" Trina's brown eyes popped wide open and she shook her head in disbelief. "After all you do, how could you not want it?"

"Join us. The job could be yours."

Trina waved her hands in the air in exasperation. "I'm not a leader, I'm a---"

"Beauty queen," Kofi answered bitterly. "What a tragic waste of your life and just between us, I think you are setting a bad example for all African-American girls, especially the beautiful ones. The message you are sending is that beauty is better than brains, that change will not come by hard work and sacrifice but by standing on stage in a swimsuit." Kofi's tone was dark. "What kind of legacy is that? Look at Michelle Obama. She's beautiful, but she always makes sure that the accent is on her intelligence." Kofi gripped Trina's hands. "You must be the Michelle Obama for school girls."

Trina snatched her hands free.

Kofi sighed. "I just hope you don't turn out to be like one of those artificial women on BET."

Trina struggled for a reply and when no words came, she walked off.

CHAPTER FOUR

The effects of being in the same room with a woman as elegant as Rosa Ebenezer had a big impact on Trina. The woman was smart and beautiful, and Trina was very impressed. Madam Rosa was someone all black women in Charlotte could be proud of.

As First Lady of the church where her husband had been the pastor since the church had been established a few years ago, Trina was tempted to compare Madam Rosa to Michelle Obama, the First Lady of the United States. Over the last few days, Michelle Obama had privately scored a lot of emotional points with Trina, who had studied the First Lady eagerly. It appeared that everything Michelle Obama had done in her life had been merely an introduction, preparation for what she was doing now. Trina was awed by how well The First Lady had learned her lessons, and then had been unafraid to translate them into action where she could help others.

"Is Michelle Obama what they call a Shero?" Trina quizzed.

Madam Rosa smiled, the dimples in her dark face deepening. "Yes." The response was fast, automatic. "For most of my life, I have had to deal with hero worship, males who did all the good and right things. During those times, women were not allowed to play big roles so we were not given much room to make our way into history, but now that has changed. Thank God. Women no longer have to labor without being compensated by history." Madam Rosa opened her arms wide in a gesture of thanksgiving. "Halleluiah", she exclaimed happily. "History will call us by name."

Trina was captivated. "What do you think I have to do to become a Shero like Michelle Obama?"

Madam Rosa's facial expression changed. "You don't have to imitate anyone to be a Shero because different women will use different ways to bring about change." She looked deep into Trina's eyes. "I agree that Mrs. Obama is a great example for all women, but Trina, there are other women that fulfill the requirements of being a Shero."

"Who?! Tell me about them?" Trina spoke excitedly.

Madam Rosa's voice became sad. "No one understands what it has been like for the black woman. No one realizes our struggle, but in spite of all our hardships, we have never stopped fighting to make our voices heard."

Hearing the excited voices, Reverend Ebenezer stuck his head into the kitchen. "What's going on in here? Sounds like a celebration to me."

Madam Rosa looked at Trina, then at her husband. "Our lips are sealed, so you can just march right on back outside and make yourself useful by doing something that men do. This kitchen is now the official center for girl talk." Madam Rosa smiled, shooing her smiling husband away.

When the Reverend had left, Madam Rosa patted Trina's hand. "Now, let's talk seriously about something that I want you to be aware of." She paused. "I just don't want you to be aware of it, but I want you to beware of it and I will then need you to make it known to other young girls, okay?'

At some deep level, Trina knew this talk would not be anything to laugh about. She braced herself emotionally.

"Have you ever hear of SIS?" When Trina admitted that she hadn't, Madam Rose continued. "SIS, stands for Strong Independent Sisters, and we are a dedicated group of black women whose primary mission is to support each other in our personal and professional lives. But that is just the start because we also attempt to strengthen our communities by establishing programs for the women and children who live there." Madam Rosa paused. "Even though the chapter here in Charlotte just started, we are very committed. Recently, we joined in the Susan B. Komen Breast Cancer Walk. We participated in the Toys 4 Tots campaign and we donated dresses that could be used by young girls on prom night."

"I think that's great. What can I do?"

"Let me ask you something, Trina. Do you ever feel blessed?"

Trina nodded.

"Now, let me ask you this. Have you ever heard of Rachel Carson or Upton Sinclair?"

This time Trina shook her head.

"Not many people have. Anyway, Rachel Carson wrote a book entitled "Silent Spring" which exposed the harmful use of pesticides and herbicides on the food we consume. The book was important in that it paved the way for the banning of harmful chemicals in our foods. Upton Sinclair was responsible for bringing about improvements in the meat-packing industry which led to safe handling of meats and poultry. What happened before these books were published was not pretty." Madam Rosa stared into the eyes of Trina. "Many people think the next big battle will be over oil, but they are wrong. The biggest battle will be over who controls the food supply because whoever wins this struggle will decide what goes into the food we put on our tables."

"Makes me want to cry," Trina confessed. "But why?"

"It's simple. Food is the most powerful commodity in the world. It is more precious than gold or diamonds." Madam Rosa groaned. "Does that make sense to you? The fast-food industry is trying to insure their future with our bellies." Madam Rosa shook her head. "They believe they can accomplish with their foodstuffs what fear and intimidation couldn't. There is a food fight going on which will lead to Armageddon."

"What do you want me to do?"'

Madam Rosa turned her back to Trina as she gathered a manila folder from a shelf. She handed it to Trina. "This is a photo of a seemingly delicious hamburger. Looks yummy, doesn't it? Look at the pickles and the lettuce, the ketchup. What you can't see is pink slime."

"*Pink slime!?*"

"Unsuspecting boys and girls, your age, have been eating it, not just at McDonalds', but in school as well."

Trina wasn't exactly sure if that was true or not, but she had a very good idea that it was."

"Such dietary trickery by these false food prophets must be stopped or more young children will end up with food-borne ailments so horrible that they will never be able to live normal lives again."

"What do you want me to do?" Trina asked for the second time.

"SIS need girls like you to act as ambassadors for healthy eating alternatives, someone who will help young teens to understand this new McDonalds' inspired world of fantasy nutrition. Children grow up with the illusion that a burger and fries possess great nutritional value when, in effect, none of this is true."

"Well, what happens next?"

Madam Rosa took a deep breath. "You get introduced to a life of dietary slavery."

"Slavery?!" Trina was jolted by the revelation. "How will that happen?"

"Hardly any of the teenagers brought up in modern-day America will escape the effects of the McDonald's syndrome so they end up fat, out of shape, and worse." Madam Rosa made a face. "You do understand what happens to these young people, don't you?"

"My goodness," Trina shrieked pitifully. "They die?"

"Eventually. But until they do, they are forced to live marginal lives because obesity and diabetes will stunt their zest for life as they are victimized by their need to rely on medications and dietary fads that never work. And that is why we must do something. We must expose and eliminate this ugly practice of selling young people a dream where visions of French fries and super-sized sodas dance in their heads." The bitterness showed in Madam Rosa's voice. "If we don't rescue them, that dream will continue to be a nightmare."

CHAPTER FIVE

Trina had never been so excited—or confused--in her life. In many ways, she was glad to help Madam Rosa, but at the same time, she felt sad because she didn't truly want to give up her personal dreams. There were still things she wanted to accomplish on her own, but should she put her private desires above the concerns of all high school girls? Would that be selfish of her? Ultimately, she would have to decide. Soon.

Without a doubt, she was sympathetic to the plight of her teenage peers. What girl wouldn't be? But at the same time she felt individually compelled to compete fully in her own dreams. Trina frowned. All her life, she had dreamed of being a beauty queen, not a female crusader for the justice of young, overweight girls in America. All the images in her head were, and always had been, of her becoming the new standard of black beauty. *And now this!*

Trina felt rattled as if life had shaken her up. Could she somehow skirt the great responsibility that had been placed on her slender shoulders? She smiled briefly, thinking that she should grab Kofi and run off into the sunset with him to live on some deserted island. She quickly shook herself free of that idea, but just as quickly thought about her parents. What about them? This was so remarkable.

After a short nap, it was clear to Trina about what she had to do. She would join SIS. Madam Rosa already had a plan where she would send one of the SIS members to work for OWN, the new television station owned by Oprah Winfrey. Madam Rosa had every intention of using the television station as a medium to open a discussion about The Cinderella Syndrome.

Trina was disturbed by The Cinderella Syndrome. She knew that in Teen-age America, many young, urban girls lived lives that were so controlled by the highly-commercialized fast-food media blitz that they did not find wholesome foods appealing. Sadly, many girls were traumatized by this multi-national food crisis because the American version of a healthy meal was imposed upon them by McDonalds and Burger King.

"You are much too young for such serious thought." Alfreda, Trina's mother, smiled as she walked into the kitchen where her daughter was boiling cassava. "You look like a stature."

Trina gazed at her mother. *"I do!"* she exclaimed, surprised that her anxiety was so visible.

"Yes, you do and I want you to tell me what's on your mind."

All at once, Trina had problems breathing, swallowing, and seeing straight. Her hands and knees both trembled uncontrollably and her face felt hot. She had never lied to her mother before.

"You think I don't know what it's like to be a teenager, my daughter? You feel like you have been robbed of your childhood identity, and now believe you must find a substitute one before you reach adulthood. It cannot be easy trying to sew together an identity from two worlds that are so different." Alfreda smiled. "I think I will stand back for now and let you fight, but I promise that I will not let you get hurt."

"But who—what—am I fighting, Mama?"

"The one thing that all people, at one time or another, fight against: that mysterious thing called not-being-enough. You know, not good enough, or not smart enough, or not pretty enough. Whatever your *"not enough"* is, in your mind you may think you are fighting for some noble cause when all you are really doing is fighting for acceptance." Alfreda paused. "It's no different for young boys who grow up seeking to win a boxing championship. They really believe they are battling other men, but they fight to secure a place where they can belong."

Trina had never known her mother to be so wise.

Alfreda hugged her daughter closely. "Lying to your mother is not the most inspirational thing you can do right now, so I'll postpone our conversation until you are really ready to tell me what is going on in your young life." Alfreda winked. "How's that?"

Trina felt such relief. For the time being, she had no choice but to continue to wrestle over how best to do what she had to do without her parents finding out. And that just might be the hardest thing she had ever had to do.

Suddenly, everything was changing and Trina felt like she was about to kiss her Plain Jane, school-girl life goodbye.

Who knew what would come next.

What happened the next day puzzled Trina. On her way home from Madam Rosa's house, she saw Kofi. She watched unnoticed as he stepped out of the front door of a small, corner store on the Eastside, and then eased into a small cluster of people before moving out into the long shadows of the early evening. She loved it when the fading sun lazily danced across the top of Kofi's head, adding a glowing spark to his dreadlocks. She also enjoyed the crazy way his face absorbed the sunlight when he squinted into the glare so that he could see into the distance. Trina figured he was searching for someone.

She ducked inside the doorway of an exotic fish store, her arms folded across her chest, her head tilted forward. Out of habit, she took a few deep breaths to clear her head. She was curious to see how long it would take Kofi to approach whomever it was he had come to see. Tracking Kofi's movement once he started moving, Trina was momentarily paralyzed as Kofi headed in the direction of a tall, pretty girl but she emitted a sigh of relief when he walked past her.

Oddly pleased that Kofi had ignored the girl, Trina noticed that the crowd of people across the street seemed to part as a very big man slowly approached Kofi from the left. The man firmly gripped Kofi's hand in greeting. Kofi smiled.

Trina quietly watched as Kofi and the man made their way to a black sedan parked on the corner where Kofi hurriedly slipped an envelope into the man's outstretched hand. The man seemed pleased. He patted Kofi on the head like a good dog. Kofi seemed pleased.

Trina ran to the bus stop.

Three blocks down the Avenue, the sleek, black sedan appeared out of nowhere, moving fast towards the intersection, but the light turned red and at the very last second, the car screeched to a halt. Peeking down into the vehicle, Trina saw two grim-faced men in the front. Alone in the backseat of the sedan was the big man whom she had seen with Kofi. The man was grinning happily as he plucked glossy photos out of the envelope Kofi had given him.

When the traffic light changed colors, the car sped off like a guided missile.

Frantic thoughts, like angry bees, swarmed Trina's mind. Something did not seem right. Instantly, her mind made all kinds of connections but none felt right. *Something was wrong!*

Before she realized it, the bus was uptown, dwarfed by the huge glass and concrete skyscrapers of Center City. At the terminal she changed buses, boarding the outbound transit that covered the Central Avenue and Eastway vicinity.

Minutes later, the big bus tore out of the terminal and was soon zooming through a no-name community where most of the red-brick apartments were boarded up with plywood. She saw both beggars and bandits.

The bus zoomed on.

Next came a row of houses, pink and pretty, where well-to-do people who were born with a silver spoon in their mouths had built a place to call home.

The bus zoomed on.

Nothing more was left of her trip home except a flower-pot plot of earth where tombstones with fancy script paid silent tribute to men and women who lay beneath the dirt.

The bus stopped.

Walking the short distance to her house, Trina gave herself permission to worry. She worried about the life she used to know. She worried about the HSC. She worried about SIS. She worried about her parents. She worried about the first day of school. But most of all, she worried about the strange men in their fancy black car. And Kofi.

The next time she saw Kofi was on a Wednesday that rained. They met in a friendly, neighborhood park on Kilborne Avenue where the wet splashes of water hung from the branches of trees like tiny, see-through balloons.

For Trina, her feelings for Kofi were not just some school-girl crush. They were much bigger and stronger than that. Simply put, she liked him a lot and for some strange reason felt like some invisible force was organizing the rest of her summer around him. It seemed so dreamy.

Standing under the shelter to stay dry, Trina had no idea when Kofi would make mention of the strange men in the fancy car and when he never did, she began to feel as if Kofi was baby-sitting her instead of being a real friend.

"If I asked you something," Trina asked calmly, "would you tell me the truth?"

"Look, Trina," Kofi said, "I'm not here to answer questions."

"Then why are you here?" Trina snapped.

"I'm here because I like you, but," Kofi paused, "I think it might be best if I leave."

Trina gripped Kofi's arm. "Don't leave. Please." At that moment, she understood that this would not be the last battle Kofi would win with her, but it didn't matter. All she knew was that she was not interested in handing him over to someone else. For all she knew, other girls waited eagerly.

Once everything had been smoothed over, Kofi was all business. "Tell you what. I'm going to explain to you about the hippos and the cheetahs."

"The hippos and the cheetahs!?"

"Yes, exactly."

As if on cue, the rain stopped and Kofi escorted Trina from the shelter out into the fresh air. The freshly-cut green grass sparkled.

"Watch your step," Trina giggled. "I don't want you to fall."

"There is an old proverb from our Motherland: *Do not look where you fell, but where you slipped.* Seeing the look of confusion on Trina's face, Kofi put his arms around her shoulder. "These days, everyone who claims they are trying to lift black America up is looking at the place where she fell down. Don't look there. Look at the place where she slipped. That is where the problem is."

"But what has any of that have to do with hippos and cheetahs?" Trina smiled. "Is this like Wiley the Coyote and the Road-runner?"

Kofi scowled. "The Road-Runner is a cartoon whereas the hippos and cheetahs represent the two classes of people who want to control the destiny of young people. The hippos are the old-fashioned ones who are stuck in the old ways. They like doing things the way they did them back in the 60s when Doctor King was alive." Kofi's eyes were fierce. "They say in the Bible that you can't pour fresh wine into old skins."

"Who are the cheetahs?" Trina inquired.

Kofi stopped and faced Trina. "The cheetahs are us. We are the cheetahs. The new generation must rule ourselves. Our ideas are fresh and new, fast. The ideas of the hippos are slow, and they must be swept out of the way. A new day has come for us. Long live the cheetahs."

CHAPTER SIX

It was impossible for Trina to believe what she was hearing. Were her ears deceiving her? Was her mind playing tricks on her? She didn't know. What she did know was that she felt like screaming and screaming.......and screaming.

Shonda was missing!

It was 11:00 on the brightest morning of the week, and Trina was back at Madam Rosa's house. Only this time, the kitchen looked like police headquarters. There were people running in and out, phones were ringing, and there was paper everywhere. Trina took it all in.

When Reverend Ebenezer came in from a side entrance, he spoke loudly. "This was a kidnapping." He sat down at the far end of the table. "And we all know who is responsible."

Madam Rosa shook her head in disgust, shocked at how easy it had been for the kidnappers to make off with Shonda. "These guys are good."

"And we are going to have to be better if we are going to rescue Shonda." Reverend Ebenezer looked at Trina. "This is the danger we were trying to warn you about." He sighed. "Plus, you may be the next target."

"Me?! Why?!"

Reverend Ebenezer sighed again. "You might as well know."

"*Know what!?*" There was fear in Trina's voice.

"Many of these so-called beauty pageants are fake. They are set up to lure young, pretty girls like Shonda into a trap where they can be kidnapped."

"But-but that can't be true," Trina protested, "because last year a woman from Angola was just crowned Miss Universe."

"That was real," Madam Rosa said. "That beauty pageant was legitimate and Leila Lopes of Angola is now indeed Miss Universe. The ones you have to be careful of are the small, local ones like the one Shonda entered."

"I know what you must be feeling," Reverend Ebezener commented, "but what is happening here in Charlotte and elsewhere across the country is that young, pretty girls are being kidnapped and whisked off to faraway places where they are forced to work in fast food restaurants."

"The black girls usually end up in Africa or the West Indies," Madam Rosa added.

"But why?" Trina cried out.

"The love of money," Reverend Ebenezer proclaimed, "but yet there is so much more, something far more sinister, something that must be stopped." He gazed at Trina. "Have you ever heard of a concept called The New World Order?"

Trina confessed that she had even though she had no idea what it meant.

"Well, what it means is that corporate America is out to remake and to reshape the world. The concept is not new and many nations have tried it, using various tactics and techniques. The sword and the gun are the usual methods, but they didn't work so well. Then hot-shot international bankers tried to unite the world under the banner of a single currency. That failed as well. Nothing worked."

"Then why are they still trying?" Trina asked. "Why don't they just give up?"

"Because they feel they have now found the solution. They want to conquer the world by taking over our stomachs. They feel that if they can control our eating habits, they can manipulate the rest of our actions." Reverend Ebenezer paused for a second. "The world is becoming smaller because of corporations like McDonalds, more mechanized. McDonalds is a major force around the globe. In India, China, Chile, Germany. In all of these countries, McDonalds set the standard for what the people eat. And that's powerful. Japanese children now shun the age-old custom of the tea ceremony, instead opting for a soda at McDonalds.

Whole cultures have been toppled by the fast food nation. Now, they have set their sights on Africa."

"B-but that's evil." Trina was disturbed. "And scary."

"Very scary, I'm afraid." Reverend Ebenezer smiled paternally. "The powers-that-be couldn't get the world to believe in the same God or the same coin or the same politics, but they are succeeding in forcing us to believe in one common dietary theme—fast food. Just think about how powerful that is. If someone can control what you eat and how you respond to what you eat, then they can control you since a large part of everyone's day is consumed either by eating or thinking about eating. As a result, a large part of our earnings goes towards satisfying our obsession with eating."

Madam Rosa shook her head. "But they want to keep us out of the kitchen and in their fast-food joints."

Trina was curious. She fought back tears. "But why did they take Shonda?"

"Okay, okay," Reverend Ebenezer said, "let me explain. "For years now, there has been a conspiracy by the fast-food industry to get rid of beauty pageants because they don't like the image. Don't get me wrong, they don't care so much about the beauty of these girls. That's not it at all. What they hate is the body of these girls. They want to promote a new national body image that is well, more...."

"Fat." Madam Rosa finished the sentence. "There's no need to play games."

Trina was stunned. "Can-can they do that?"

"Why not?" Reverend Ebenezer asked. "In the same way that they engineered the 'thin-is-in' concept a while back where they had young girls suffering from anorexia and bulimia to fit the image, no doubt women will soon feel comfortable about being overweight."

"You must never underestimate the power of Hollywood and the media," Madam Rosa warned sternly. "A whole generation of black women were traumatized in the 60s by not feeling pretty enough all because they didn't—couldn't--fit the Barbie Doll image. Talk about low self-esteem."

"And now the same thing is happening again?"

"Yes, Trina, I'm afraid, it is." Madam Rosa sighed. "There's a lot at stake, the whole world is up for grabs and corporate America wants it. What's even more scary is that in the same way that the fast-food industry found a way to process burgers and fries, they want to manufacture processed people in the same way."

"How?!"

"Through the use of genetically modified foods. Burger joints needs tons of potatoes and tomatoes, so the industry along with bio-tech companies are searching for a way to inject these foods with a synthetic gene that will make humans more docile and passive." Reverend Ebenezer laughed bitterly. "They want to process out our innate intelligence and produce a nation of passive slaves."

"They must be stopped," Trina remarked.

"One thing I know," said Reverend Ebenezer, "is that the local police are not going to be any better at solving this case than they were with solving the last ones." He stood tall. "If we are going to stop this kidnapping ring, we must do it ourselves or else we lose Trina next."

Trina gasped.

"That's not happening. Nothing or no one will touch my daughter."

Trina snapped to attention when her father entered the kitchen. She ran to him, hugging him tightly. "What are you doing here?"

Reverend Ebenezer laughed. "Your father is a part of our secret police force."

"And that's why you didn't want me to enter the beauty---?"

"No. I did that because I love you. I was just doing my job as a father." Turning his attention to the men assembled, Trina's father spoke confidently. "What I have been able to establish is that we have a bad apple in our midst. Someone is not only helping the kidnappers, but is also helping to deliver the girls to them by gaining their trust. His usual method is to turn the girls against their parents, then he convinces them to run off with him."

"Then what happens?" Trina asked.

"What happens next, Princess," Trina's father replied, "is that the girls are then sold into fast-food slavery."

"I want the name of this-this traitor," Reverend Ebenezer shouted.

"What good will a name do?" Trina's father said. "We need to get on the inside."

"It's too risky."

Just then another man Trina knew from church rushed in. "I have a photo. It was faxed to me by a Nigerian friend of mine whose niece was taken last year." He passed the picture to the reverend, who glared at it for a second before plopping it down on the kitchen table. "Has anyone seen this man?"

When Trina cried out, everyone knew that she had seen him.

"You-you know him?" her father asked.

Trina breathlessly explained that the man in the photo was the same man who had been in the black car. She also explained that she had seen him with some photos. What she didn't mention was that the man had gotten the photos from Kofi.

Thirty minutes later, Reverend Ebenezer had found out who the man in the photo was.

"They call him The King."

For the first time since she had met Kofi, Trina paid more attention to what her head was telling her than her heart because if Kofi was the traitor in the community and was working with the slavery ring, she had every reason to be careful.....and scared.

She prayed that she was wrong about Kofi because if she wasn't that would mean she had been living in a make-believe fantasy world when all he had wanted to do was to sell her like a fish at an open air bazaar. In any event, she was going to find out.

Knowing that nothing good would come out of a full-scale argument with Kofi, she decided she would have to use a different theme. Just what, she had no clue. Not yet anyway. Even though she knew she was better suited to being a beauty queen than a private eye, her mind was made up. This was her war and she was going to win. Somehow. Some way.

Girl-Power!

Suddenly, Trina felt like Queen Candace, the Kushite Queen, that even Alexander the Great refused to fight. As a little girl, Trina remembered her father telling about the African queen who had forced Alexander to retreat. After Alexander and his armies had conquered Egypt, he decided to invade Kush, but when he was met at the border by Queen Candace and her troops, Alexander thought better of tangling with the black queen. He hurriedly turned around and took his business elsewhere. *No one messed with the Queen!*

The story inspired her as did the story of another African woman, Queen Nzinga, who fought against the Portuguese who wanted to enslave her people. Queen Nzinga wasn't having it. She was a brilliant warrior who fought against slavery until she died at eighty years old.

And now it was her turn to battle wrong.

Enter Queen Trina!

The stories of the African queens made her bolder and she smiled. Her enemies had just picked up the other end of the stick. What they saw was the end with the beauty queen on it. What they never saw was the other end where there was a warrior queen!

Later that night as she sat at her computer, Trina wondered how to go about her new duties. By now, she was really feeling the power of what she was doing and she was eager to arm young, black girls with a new infusion of hope. When she was finished, she wanted black beauty and strength to be celebrated. She also wanted to establish a lot of programs to help young, inner-city girls find their places in a fast-food world, but the project she would advocate strongest was one where girls learned that beauty was not as great a survival tool as brains, and that what went into their stomachs was just as important as what went into their minds.

When she finally clicked the computer OFF, she got the same feeling that Reverend Ebenezer had spoken of earlier. *They were alone!* Stories about missing black girl was not front page news. Rubbing the sleep from her weary eyes, she didn't know whether to laugh or to cry over her new adventure.

In any event, she knew she was going to bed for the last time as a helpless young girl.

Tomorrow she would be reborn.

BOOK TWO

CHAPTER SEVEN

Trina pretended not to notice the sinking feeling in her stomach as she watched Kofi coming towards her.

"Where's my hug?' he commented calmly,

Trina turned away, saying nothing.

"I thought we were closer than that?"

"We are."

"Well, you've got a strange way of showing it."

Trina ignored the biting rebuke for a second before turning on the charm. "I'm just playing with you, boy." She giggled as she embraced Kofi warmly. Then she switched topics. "My friend, Shonda, is missing." She studied Kofi's reaction. "No one knows where she is."

Kofi squeezed Trina's hand gently. "I hate to hear that. I feel sorry for you."

"*Me?!*" Trina blurted without thinking.

"I feel sorry for your friend, but I feel sorry that you have lost her. I know how I would feel if a friend of mine was kidnapped."

Instantly, a red light came ON in Trina's head. Kofi had expressed sympathy for her rather than for Shonda.

"What makes you think she was kidnapped? I simply said she was missing."

Kofi shrugged. "That's how it usually goes. Boys go missing. Girls get kidnapped."

Carefully observing the features of Kofi's smooth, dark face, Trina watched as a wide smile brightened the twinkle in his brown eyes. She walked backwards, studying him like he was a lab specimen.

"Why you walking like that? You might fall or something."

Trina thought it was pure genius. This way she wouldn't miss anything. She felt that was important since she had read somewhere that the eyes were the window to a person's soul and she felt that if she couldn't read Kofi's mind, his soul might be the next best place to look. Anything to give her a more revealing look into any part of the man—if Kofi was that man— that many considered a traitor.

Keeping in mind that she could be next in line to come up missing, Trina honestly believed that she had to invest every ounce of her energy into her investigation. She understood that she couldn't let up if she wanted to get the scoop on who the big man—The King—was. But she also knew that she couldn't get careless. This, after all, was no National Geographic documentary or After-School Special. If she was going to blow the lid off The King's scheme to rule the world, she had to stay alive because death was not a passing grade. Trina wanted to graduate.

In her mind, she knew, without a doubt, that it was much too late for her to count on her experience as an investigator. For starters, she had none. In fact, this was her very first interrogation even if the subject, Kofi, had no idea that he was being grilled.

Turning herself around, she informed herself that she did have some background in this field. She smiled. She had watched The No. 1 Ladies' Detective Agency twice. That may not have given her an A-1 reputation, but it was a place to click her heels.

Once she got going, it was hard for her to slow down with the questions, but she softened her voice so it wouldn't seem like she was plucking a chicken clean for the market although a few times it did come close to that.

"You talking a lot today, but it's all good because I enjoy hearing your voice." Kofi winked slyly. "And to my knowledge, that may not be the wisest thing to tell a woman. Just kidding," he quickly added. "Just kidding."

Meeting his gaze, Trina spoke solemnly. "Give me your honest opinion. Do you think Shonda is still alive?"

Kofi's eyes flashed. "Don't worry. If she is, the police will find her. That's what they get paid to do, you know?' He put his arm around Trina's shoulder. "At least now, you wouldn't have any competition if you did enter the beauty pageant."

That remark angered Trina. "So you think that Shonda is prettier than me? You think that I couldn't have won if I had to compete against her? Maybe that is the reason no one, including you, wanted me to enter the contest," she huffed. "No one felt I was pretty enough to win. Thanks."

"Trina, please come to your senses. You are the most beautiful girl in the world. You have no competition. Know why? Because nothing compares to you." Kofi appeared lost in thought. "You know what? The only reason I was dead set against you entering the pageant is because I thought you could better serve the people by being a woman of intellect, but now that I think about it, it just might be a good idea for you to enter the contest." After a slight pause, he added. "You really do need to get it out of your system."

"I do, do I?" A trace of sarcasm colored Trina's tone, "I'm honored that all of a sudden, you believe that I could change the world by winning a beauty contest when before now you---"

"Look, Trina, can we please talk about something else? Since I'm driving today, why don't you let me treat you to a big ol' banana split at Dairy Queen."

"Okay, and maybe while we're over there, I can compete with the cow for her crown."

"What?!"

"Since I need to get this out of my system, like you say, I think I will challenge all the queens for their titles. Start off at Dairy Queen and then work my way up to the Queen of England."

"On second thought," Kofi commented, "why don't I just take you to Burger King."

Back in her headquarters, which is now what Trina called her bedroom, she had somehow stumbled upon the concept that if she could keep the fire burning under Kofi that he would soon crack like Humpty-Dumpty. Plus, there were some other people she felt she needed to shake up. She turned on her TV to watch 'Law and Order' in the hopes of getting an insider's view of the relationship between a good investigator and a tough criminal. She strongly believed that watching cop shows on the tube counted as online experience because the more you watched, the more you knew.

Sitting in the lotus position so she could better absorb the perplexities of the learning curve, Trina hoped that Kofi could take it as well as he could dish it out because she was going to burst him like a pus-filled bump. Ugh! Who said what she had to do was going to be pleasant.

At the conclusion of her "online education" Trina switched the television OFF and flopped back on her bed, silent. She managed to take one or two quick breaths in a failed attempt to rush more oxygen to her brain. She felt numb. She hoped it was because she was learning so much so quickly because her whole purpose, among other things, was to bring the kidnappers of Shonda to justice. The sooner, the better.

The more she had learned about the way crimes got solved, the clearer it became that the wheels were already turning at a fast pace, pumping and churning in favor of the crooks who mostly eluded capture if they made it past the first 48 hours. That sickened her because she was already late. She was going to play this game by her own rules which she felt was best since she didn't know what the rules were in the first place.

Trina dived under the covers. Even Sheroes needed to sleep

.

"Wow!" Trina shrieked in delight.

It was mid-morning with plenty of sunshine outside but hardly any light inside her bedroom except the artificial glare thrown off by her pair of computers. She was gathering data. No more FaceBook. No more MySpace. No more YouTube.

Just then, 'the information center' where the computers and borrowed fax machine were kept, became active. More requested data was being faxed in. She hummed anxiously as the machine whirred, spewing forth the incoming info and when it finally ended, her face twisted into a frown. She had struck out once more. This was not news she could use. She made a silly face at the fax machine. She still had options. She just had to think more creatively.

Thirty minutes later, her phone rang again.

"That didn't work," she groaned. "Got anything else?"

"Come on, Trina," Geek, the computer whiz kid on the other end of the line, cracked. "I'm just getting

\\\started. What's wrong, you think I'm a one trick pony or something?"

"Don't know about that, but maybe you're an old dog that can't learn new tricks."

"Ha!" Geek, a native American laughed. "Hold on, sista, slow down. I invented the tricks."

"Well, what I'm telling you is that there is someone else out there who is breathing down your neck."

Geek became thoughtful. "That system I gave you worked perfectly last summer when I needed to find out who was trying to shakedown my tribe's gambling casino in Connecticut. Maybe what you've got is a smokescreen."

"A smokescreen? What's that?"

"It's what happens when you can't uncover what you what to uncover because of walls and layers put in place to protect the info you are trying to uncover. Follow me?"

"Of course I do. Well, I think I do. Anyway, if someone is clever enough to fix a smokescreen, how do we smoke them out."

"Good question."

"And the answer is....?"

Without bothering to reply, Geek faxed Trina another set of his special 'computer coordinates'. When he was sure that Trina had them, he breathlessly announced. "People would wrestle an alligator to get what you've just got."

"Is it what the doctor ordered?" Trina teased.

"Better," Geek bragged. "This is better than any order, prescription, or hocus-pocus. This is real magic. Try it. You can thank me later. Bye."

Even though she knew she might not get much, the idea of getting anything at all struck her as good as the pot of gold at the rainbow's end. Yet she refused to get caught up in the notion of what could be. Instead she stared at the link Geek had sent her, attempting to interpret the value of the info. Nothing was revealed. In short, it was nothing more than a long line of computer spaghetti and so it would remain until she ran the link and clicked on it.

She began to enter the info into her computer. "*Let's get busy!*" she told herself.

Nothing happened.

Disappointed, Trina had had enough. As she dressed, she examined her shadow on the bedroom wall. When she was completely dressed, she walked shakily to the mirror to see if she looked like she felt. Thank God, she didn't.

Realizing that she had been right all along, she didn't have to imagine what she would do next. Call Geek and let him know that he was a computer whiz-kid has-been. She sighed. This was not the first time she had to burst someone's bubble. Probably wouldn't be her last.

Her phone rang and to her surprise, it was Geek. "May I speak to the lady who will be the lady of the house in about twenty more years?"

"Boy----"

"Type in my name, G-E-E-K, at the end of the link and then it's on."

Breathing raggedy, Trina shouted. "Why didn't you tell me that to begin with?"

"Because I wanted you to feel the power."

Racing back to the information center, Trina punched in the four letters, then clicked on the link. After a second or two, she made an entry in her journal. *I KNOW WHO THE KING IS!!!*

CHAPTER EIGHT

Now, Trina had a big decision to make. Did she tell Reverend Ebenezer what she had found out. Although it wasn't a part of her original plan, it did make sense. She wondered what Ice-T or Precious Ramotswe would do? More than likely, they would choose to unravel the scheme on their own....solo. There. It was settled.

But she had to trust someone. She knew it was a long shot, but Geek was the only person she felt she could trust. Now, it was *really* settled.

She called her friend. "Can I buy you lunch?"

"It'll never work."

"What won't work, silly?"

"Whatever it is you're trying to bribe me into helping you with unless, that is, you let me choose two desserts."

"Done," Trina remarked merrily. "You have got yourself a deal. Meet me at McDonalds."

"*McDonalds?!*"

Trina giggled cheerfully. "Times are tough and money is hard to come by. I'll make it up to you later. Plus, I want to personally see what pink slime looks like."

"Famous last words," Geek lamented. "As due compensation, I'm going to have to request a toy with my Happy Meal."

"If we get there in time, I might be able to get you some leftover promotional stuff."

"Pokemon?"

"The possibility is intriguing."

"How many?"

"All seven figures. All twelve cards."

"How?!"

"I got people," Trina chirped. "You think you're the only one that can make it do what it do?"

As she watched Geek eat, Trina tried to erase the image of Shonda from her mind, but the effort failed. In her head, she still had a bird's eye view of what Shonda was going through and what could be next for her if she didn't make some progress soon. Thanks to her lunch companion and soon-to-be partner, she also knew that The King didn't play around. Neither did it thrill her to know that The King's idea of conflict resolution wasn't taught at Harvard, Yale, or Johnson C. Smith University. Evidently, he and Hannibal Lecter had studied together.

Trina shook in her boots. She still had a lot of reasons to worry.

"Oh boy," she said, "do I have something to tell you."

Probably what shocked Geek most about the vivid conversation he was having with his friend was that it gave him little to smile about.

"*Are you crazy?!* Geek exploded.

Other than that outburst, Trina never gave him another chance to interrupt her, and by the time she was finished spinning her story, she looked almost too embarrassed to repeat her earlier request for help, but she had no choice.

"I need you to be my partner."

Geek cleared his throat. "I'm afraid that we have somehow landed on different pages. I thought that maybe you wanted to find The Wizard of Oz, not the Master of Disaster. Don't get me wrong," Geek pleaded, "and go to thinking that I don't appreciate lunch, but believe me, it's not me you need. Who you need is that very bad man on 'Breaking Bad'. He's a perfect candidate for the job. Does this kind of stuff every episode."

Trina deliberately kept her voice calm. "You the man."

"Can't say that that's not true," Geek patiently explained, "but I am man of peace, a man of techno-gizmos, and one day I hope to be the man of some household. However, I am not and I repeat, I am not the man for this job. In fact, I'm feeling very boyish right now."

"You know what, Geek? I guess I'm the only one that can see the real you. The man in you has been idling, just waiting for someone like me to come along with a scheme such as the one I just presented to you so you can be released from your geekiness."

Geek wiped bread crumbs from his upper lip and pondered that statement. "Rarely, if ever, has two things, such as what you believe you see in me and what I want to believe about myself been more far apart. I sincerely apologize if I sound unsympathetic, but let me be the first to tell you that you have fallen victim to a fairytale."

Trina pointed her finger. "Man up, Geek!"

"Okay, okay, but if I die, would you make sure that Lady GaGa sings 'Born This Way' at my funeral?"

"You're not going to die, Geek."

"Well, until I get it in writing from The King, I'll keep my fingers crossed." Geek winced. "How often does lunch turn into an invitation to a premature death?" He grinned wickedly. "Let's get it on!"

Trina instantly turned ON the charm. After getting in line at the Corner Store where she had seen Kofi on the day he had met The King, she made no mistake about where she was. She was well aware that this store was a hub for illegal activity.

Geek watched her back as other men came in from the drizzle, bounding in off the sidewalk and into the premises where a burly African with a thick beard sat in a chair near the entrance, watching everyone intently. Upon a signal, he allowed certain men to pass through a metal detector in the rear of the store before gaining access to a back room. The man listened for any beeps. There were none.

At the candy counter, Trina stepped out of the line leading to the cash register and merged into the one at the metal detector, but when she was about two arms length away from it, the burly man confronted her.

"Where do you think you going?"

Trina shrugged casually. "I'm just waiting in line like everybody else."

"Well, cutie-pie, you're in the wrong line. Now, get back in the other one."

"What's this line for?"

"Am I going to have to ask you to leave?" The man scowled, didn't blink.

Jumping back into the right line, Trina paid for her groundnut toffee peanut cake and left. Geek was at her side.

Thrilled that Geek had taken pictures with his cell phone, Trina escorted Geek back to his car where they drove off in a hurry. Carefully measuring her words, she posed the question that bothered her most.

"What do you think? Did anything criminal appear to be going on?"

"Hard to tell, but I did get the feeling that something was going on. Why the metal detector?" Geek frowned. "The action is in the back, but unless I build a computer like the one they use on the TV show 'Person of Interest' to predict crime, I guess we'll never know."

"There is another way. We could break into the store."

Geek laughed loudly. "That's the craziest idea you have had yet, and trust me, you have come up with a lot of them in the last forty-eight hours. Sorry, my friend, but you can cancel that one but don't hesitate to let me know if something more sane---like calling this off--- comes up."

It was only after she had reached the relative safety and comfort of home that the graphics of the photos Geek had snapped receded enough where she once again tried to figure out a reason for all the tight security at the Corner Store. Something was definitely going on!

What she had learned so far was that the store had always served as a gathering place for African males, mainly from Nigeria. What she suspected was that the store was currently used as a network for The King.

Just as she had finished changing out of what she called her 'Shero gear' and into her well-worn cotton sweats, she studied the images of the patrons in the store that Geek had sent to her phone over again. She held them up to the light, searching for clues she might have missed before. Finding nothing, she had to assume, for the sake of argument, that the Corner Store was just what it was supposed to be----a store.

But she knew better!

Three days later.

As soon as Trina stepped out of her front door and spotted Geek, she tried to read the expression on his face, but the closer she got too where he sat in his car, she could tell the information was not good. She fought back a scream.

Driving away, Trina could see that the sun was finally breaking through the patch of clouds that had earlier covered the Eastside like a white lab coat, but all she felt was a cold chill. Beating the cross-town traffic, they pulled up across the street from the Corner Store in record time and both she and Geek watched as bumper-to-bumper traffic zoomed past. No one stopped.

"Did you get a good night's sleep last night?" Trina scolded herself for not being more polite when she had met and greeted Geek, but she had been more interested in what he had come up with. "We struck out, huh?"

Before answering, Geek shook his head. "We didn't strike out because The King and his goons do use the store to conduct their business. I did a surface check on The King and he is in this country illegally, but that's just the icing on the cake. The man is bad news." Geek's voice dropped to almost a whisper. "Food advocacy groups feels that he is the one orchestrating the disappearance of young, black girls as well as being the invisible hand behind the food modification project. It has been going on for quite a while, but the cops haven't been able to come up with anything on him." Geek smirked. "I think The KIng keeps records of everything stored away in that back room at the store."

"Man," Trina remarked hotly, "we have got to find a way to get inside that back room." She glanced at Geek. "What do you think?"

"I don't know what to think any more than you do, but the one thing I do know is that we have got to get inside that back room!"

CHAPTER NINE

Trina shivered at the thought of what the night might bring. Seated inside the cramped quarters of her 'information center' she went over the plans she had discussed with Geek who had taken it upon himself to assemble a "geek squad". Their primary job would be to enter the back room of the Corner Store.

Right away, she had some major concerns because she knew the Africans would be hard to fool. Not only that but Geek had discovered that the store was wired like a fortress and was equipped with state-of-the-art security cameras. For her own safety, she would take no part in the adventure, but she still was worried. No matter how smart and efficient the geek squad was, they would have to operate in an environment where they would have to constantly adjust their plans. Could a bunch of teenage geeks be that good?

Trina was amazed at how her life had changed. Not once in her seventeen years did she ever expect to have to view herself as a master spy, but here she was. *Life happens.* You just have to roll with the punches because sometimes destiny will recruit you to do things you never knew you could do. Still, this episode had come out of nowhere.

When Geek called, she answered without delay.

"You mentioned a link earlier," she said. "Can you tell me more?"

"Of course. Ever heard of The Sons of Isis?"

Trina had never heard of them.

"They're like the new kids on the block," Geek explained. "And when I say kids, that's what I mean. They're our age, but they're in deep. They are a bunch of pretty boys who work for The King."

"But I thought the whole operation was about pretty girls, not pretty boys."

"I'm getting to that. The pretty boys are like cheese---"

"*Cheese?!*"

"Yes, cheese, the stuff used to catch mice," Geek lectured. "Anyway, the pretty boys are the lure used to get inside the pretty girls' head. Their job is to sell the girls a dream big enough or grand enough to produce a wedge between the girls and their parents. This way, by challenging the girls' family values as old-fashioned, it makes it easier for them to trick the unsuspecting girls into running away. And here's the good part. Well, it's good for The King because if the girls run away on their own, it's not kidnapping!"

Trina mouth was a dry as cotton. The Hottentot Venus Syndrome was alive and well. Apparently, it was working as well now as it had been when Saarjtie Baartman fell for it a long, long time ago. Trina got madder at the pretty boys than she was with The King, but all of them would feel her wrath equally.

"What set these guys apart," Geek explained, "is that they don't just talk the talk. They can walk the walk. And get this. The King is so obsessed with turning out professional lures that he has established an academy where the pretty boys are coached and trained in the fine art of leading young girls astray. It seems that all the pretty boys have a passion for their work and are paid handsomely."

Trina was furious, but being angry was not a solution to her problems so she calmed down. She had no idea that The King's set-up was so detailed and so elaborate. She shook her head. What a waste of such valuable talent. In the same way the pretty boys were trained to mislead young, urban girls, they could use those same skills of persuasion to convince them to go to college to become lawyers, doctors, or nurses. She felt herself getting mad again. This was so absurd.

"I'm going to send you some photos of a couple of the pretty boys. Trina," he warned, "please don't drool on your phone, okay?"

"I-I don't need---"

"Yes, you do. You need to see these guys. Real eye candy. Any young girl would find it hard to resist the likes or the looks of guys like Kodjo Annan, Ebo Omar, and Kofi Nkurmah."

Trina gasped loudly. "Who-who did you just say? Th-that last name."

"Oh, him. Kofi Nkurmah. Ever heard of him?" Geek chuckled. "According to his profile, his trophy line is to entice girls into believing they can be a leader or a great politician. Like all the others, he's a hunk and like all the others gets a great deal of emotional satisfaction from his work. I sure wouldn't want you to run into him."

When the phone conversation ended, Trina knew that the smart thing to do would be to shake it off like a boxer who had just taken a left hook to the jaw, but she couldn't seem to snap out of it. *Kofi!* Suddenly the fact that he was a traitor bothered her more than anything else in the world with the minor exception that he was going to catch and sell her. That caused her to question everything she had ever learned about trust and human nature. Soon, she would give him something to think about.

Feeling certain that Kofi and "the pretty boys" were about to face the music, she kicked off her shoes and poured herself a glass of mango juice. At last, she felt this chapter of her life was about to close as the epic battle between brains and beauty played itself out.

Geek and the Geek Squad would not let her down.

When the fax machine whirred ON twenty minutes later, Trina almost tripped over her own feet as she dashed to retrieve the data. For some reason, she knew it was more bad news from Geek. *"Please, let me be wrong",* she prayed.

At first, she wanted to try to trick herself into believing the info was a bad dream, but after a few seconds, knew she had to accept it.

She called Geek.

"Good stuff, eh?" Geek chuckled.

Trina groaned. "Too good. If this is true, then the pretty boys pose more of a threat that we thought."

"Great observation. According to this new data, they are more like a sleeper cell than a fraternity of pretty faces because everywhere they have shown up, there has been an increase in missing girls which is what we already knew."

"So what else is new?"

79

"Guess what happens to the pretty boys once they turn a certain age deemed too old to bait teenage girls?"

"Are they shot?"

Geek laughed. "No way. What happens upon retirement is that the pretty ones are given official positions in governments throughout Africa."

"You're kidding, right?"

"Sorry, but no. What this means is that now instead of corrupting young girls, The King uses the guys to corrupt governments. I'm certain that some of the former pretty boys are in a position of high rank in some African governments where they do the bidding of their boss, The King, who has taught them everything. Pretty clever, if I do say so myself. These guys know what they are doing."

In a flash, Trina was beginning to get the whole picture. She was sure that if you tracked the collapse of some of the governments in Africa, more than likely, you would find the name of one or more of the pretty boys. Trina couldn't quite grasp the scope of it all. The King collected governments in much the same way he collected girls.

And he was on the prowl again.

The pale glow of the streetlight outside of the Corner Store sliced through the darkness, parting the blackness, casting a haunted, yellow glow across the empty parking lot. The moon lay nestled against the sky, a distant and brooding balloon.

This was the moment of truth, the point of no return, and Geek's heart skipped a beat when a police car cruised past the intersection. He immediately regained control of the situation and flashed an "all clear" sign to the other members of his crew. And just like that, the Geek Squad was ready for action.

Geek crawled to the edge of the driveway where a pair of artificial shrubs had been planted. He wasn't fooled. He knew they were not for decoration. Each contained a micro-camera that scanned the area behind the red-brick building as it was approached from the side street next to the dumpster. Several feet farther, one of his geeks flashed a signal from a northeasterly direction. The security camera on the front of the building had been disabled.

One second passed, then another two. Finally, Geek got the signal he had hoped for. The cameras in the shrubs were no longer active. Next, Geek was on his knees crawling like a baby across a path of smooth, dry sand. The path he followed seemed to vee into a crossroad of dirt and grass that was still damp from the rain earlier in the evening.

So far. So good. Geek felt lucky.

When the other two geeks, Georgie and Leo, were in place, Geek went to work on opening the lock, recalling precisely how to do it from the info on his computer. He inserted the makeshift key into the small slot in the bottom of the lock, then added some silicone. After a moment, he poured in a lead solution which had to set.

To Geek, the wait---a mere ten seconds---seemed like a daisy chain of minutes looped one around the other, but when he turned the key, all he heard was the precise clicking of the lock being released from its housing unit. He twisted the knob.

When the door opened, Geek carefully noted how it dipped to the left, creaking on its ancient hinges before rising over the sloping floor paneling. They were in, but Geek and Georgie halted while Leo aimed a scanning device to see if the floor was armed with a motion sensor. As expected, it was.

In total, the room was armed with at least five different sensors, each of them wired to a different alarm device. The Geek Squad quickly recognized the obstacles they would face in their attempt to dismantle the alarms, but they all knew that unless they could shut off the sensors, the mission would grind to a complete standstill.

Donning special goggles, Geek studied the backroom and could now easily see the brightly-colored sensor lights that illuminated the floor and walls, each arming a separate location in the room. Deciding, after only a few seconds, to continue the mission, Geek motioned for Leo to stick a pin camera into a wall socket after it had been 'cleaned'. When activated, it would let Trina see exactly what they were doing from her computer.

"Ready."

Geek nodded promptly. "Activate." After a second, he spoke into his mouthpiece. "Lady Bug, come in if you hear me."

"I'm here and I can see everything. Wow!" Trina exclaimed, "you did it. You're in. Ugh, what's up with the lights?"

"Laser beams. We can't go anywhere until we shut them down."

"Can you?"

"Every situation is different, but if anyone can put them to sleep, it's Georgie. Cross your fingers."

Ever since entering the backroom, Geek had mentally picked at his one remaining option. If, for some reason, Georgie could not deliver, he would have to perform a smash and grab. This meant that he would smash open the desk and grab whatever papers he could. This, he knew, would be a hit-or-miss operation because of the time factor. He might grab something Trina could use. He might not. What he did understand was that if he was caught, The King would ship him off to some remote place and try him for war crimes. Geek hoped that it wouldn't come to that.

It wouldn't. A second later when the laser beams fizzled out, Geek sighed in relief. "Proceed to phase two," he ordered.

Against a backdrop of semi-darkness, the Geek Squad practically pranced across the floor while Trina watched the tennis shoe ballet until they reached a silver file cabinet next to a desk. Georgie attacked the security device on the desk while Geek opened his tool kit, removing a micro-thin screw-driver from a sleeve on the left of the center tray.

Using his sense of touch as a guide, Geek inserted the screw-driver into the metal head of the screws that held the back of the file cabinet in place. While twisting the screws out, he glanced over to see that Georgie had already completed his mission. Leo was busy snapping photos of all the documents inside.

Removing the entire back panel, Geek slowly laid it aside and used his fingers to grope around inside, feeling for any surveillance devices. When nothing was found, Georgie was at his elbow, ready to make photocopies of whatever Geek handed him.

Trina's breath was trapped in her throat as she felt time come to a slow crawl. This was taking forever, it seemed, and she felt so much better when Geek gave her the thumbs-up sign. Once everything was replaced and the room restored to its normal operating conditions, the Geek Squad would leave. She fell back on her bed, a blissful grin plastered on her happy face. Now, she had the home-court advantage!

CHAPTER TEN

For the second time in the last few hours, Geek felt blessed. He stood next to Trina with a bulging-out-at-the-corner-of-his-mouth grin. He had never before experienced such a sense of accomplishment. *The Geek Squad was the bomb!*

Trina nodded, feeling what her friend felt. *The Geek Squad was the bomb!* She had already gone through the data a number of times and she was still amazed at what it all meant. She happily yanked a single sheet from the stack and waved it around like a flag.

"A'int no stopping us now," she squealed.

Geek chose not to answer. They were just a pair of kids who were no longer splashing around innocently in the shallow end of the pool. Right now, they could very well be in hot water up to their necks because The King was a living, breathing evil action figure. Nothing more. Nothing less. *Evil!*

"I just hope you know what you're in for," Geek said at last. "This is a lot bigger than missing girls, Trina, or bad cafeteria food. The King collects African governments like I used to collect baseball cards."

"I know what he does," Trina snapped. "I can read." She paused. "But aren't you curious?"

"I guess I am," Geek confessed. "I don't like what is happening and I was up all night, thinking, but this is a job for the international police." He slipped Trina a piece of paper. "Call this number and turn everything over to them. Let them bring this monster down."

Trina bit her bottom lip. "I'm sorry, Geek. I can't. This is my war. I can't let someone else fight my battles for me."

Geek stood. He hugged Trina. "Good luck, Lady Bug."

On the 20th of July, Trina met Kofi for lunch at Wendy's and his good looks almost disrupted her plans to try to flush him out as one of the pretty boys. She stared in total fascination as he poked through his salad, his beautiful face calm and serene.

"Hmm," Trina said, "that salad must be good." Pretending not to be interested, she resumed her questioning. "Tell me about your friends? What kind of man was your father?"

Kofi pushed his food aside. "Why are you wanting to know about my family and friends?"

"I thought it would be much nicer than asking about your girlfriends, don't you think?"

"I don't have a girlfriend." Kofi flexed his muscles. "I think I have already explained that to you or do you just want to hear me repeat how I believe that you are the only girl in the world for me. That's it, isn't it? You want me to expound upon all your wonderful qualities. Well," he sighed, "where shall I begin?"

Acting slightly offended, Trina teased. "You know I'm not all that."

"Trust me, Trina, you are. All I'm trying to say is that you can have anything in life. Just let me help you. I see what you don't see when you look into the mirror. You see only great beauty. I see the beauty of greatness."

"And you can help take me to the next level?"

Kofi removed his sunglasses. "I think you are a natural born leader, but you're afraid to trust your instincts. Why don't you run for the presidency of the HSC just to get your pretty feet wet? I want you to see how easy it is."

Trina shrugged. "I don't know."

Kofi's whole demeanor changed. "You're a cheetah, Trina, just like me. We were born to rule the world."

"Then why don't I feel it?"

"Don't take this the wrong way because I have nothing personal against your parents, but they're hippos and they have taught you to believe in a way of life that has no meaning in a modern society. You must free yourself."

"How?"

"By trusting me."

Trina had to fight against the urge to throw herself at Kofi's proposal. She felt weak. "Excuse me, I have to go the restroom." Dashing off to the bathroom, she splashed cold water on her face. She was falling for Kofi's line even though she knew better. She wondered if the pretty boys were hypnotists because that is exactly how she felt, like she was being hypnotized. Maybe she should command Kofi to put his sunglasses back on. If not that, then she should refuse to stare into his beautiful, brown eyes.

Annoyed at herself for acting in such a silly way, Trina gave herself a pep talk, but still the picture that Kofi presented was too much to ignore. He was like a glamour photo in the flesh. His clothes were perfect, his skin was flawless, his haircut was fresh, his nails were clean, and his voice was as soothing as an African lullaby.

Back at the table, she faced Kofi, speaking in a low tone. "I am ready for change."

After lunch, Kofi bragged. "You may get a lot of cute girls , but I just trapped Trina Brown, the beauty queen, and she is better than all of your catches combined." He pounded his chest. "I'm the baddest trapper of all times. Wow!"

The other pretty boy screwed up his face in envy. "You did well, my comrade, but if I could have gone after her, it wouldn't have taken me so long."

"And I bet you believe that?"

"It's true," Ofari contended. "Trapping girls is so easy for me." A look of pure contentment spread across his face. "You see the work I did with Shonda, the other beautiful one. I got rid of her with no problem. That's real game. You...you just got lucky. Beginner's luck, that's what it was, beginner's luck."

"Who are you after now?"

"A cutie from Ghana ."

"Heard they were easy."

Ofari looked down his nose at Kofi. "For me, all of them are easy. Remember that, okay?"

"Okay, okay, take it easy. Whatever you say." Kofi changed the subject. "I have always wondered---"

"Wondered what? What happens to the girls. That's not your cross to bear, so don't sweat it. You just do your job, collect your money, and enjoy the finer things of life. What could be better than that?'

Kofi didn't know.

At three o'clock on Tuesday, Trina locked herself in her room and for the first time instructed her mother that she did not wish to be disturbed for any reason until her guest arrived.

She was amped. Things were moving too fast and she had no way to slow them down. Sitting in the info center, she sifted through all the info she had gathered to see if he had missed anything. She hadn't.

By 3:45pm, she was sure she had positively identified five more top-ranking members of The King's organization, and though she was unsure about a sixth person, she knew the man was connected. All the signs were there so she circled the man's name to remind herself to do some more checking.

To ease the tension in her neck, she rubbed her shoulders roughly. As far as she knew, the break-in had not been detected which meant that her scheme had not been compromised, but she knew that things could still get crazy. She wished she could have gotten a whiff of this earlier so she wouldn't feel like she was racing against the clock because it was now time to get down to business.

As impressive as her feats were so far, she was wise enough to understand that there was no way she could pull her little episode off without placing herself in great danger which also meant she would be putting Shonda as well as the other girls in jeopardy. She had vowed not to let anything happen to her friends. She just prayed that this would be a promise she could keep.

Just to be on the safe side, she dug through her data again to make sure that none of the pretty boys had reached any premature conclusions about her. Nothing had been reported---yet. It appeared that none of them, Kofi included, had not seen anything suspicious enough to spill any ink on, so she exhaled.

At 4:15, there was a knock on his door. She quickly ushered the visitor in and slammed the door.

Looking across the desk, Reverend Ebenezer's eyes were as big as a pair of silver dollars. "You know where the kidnapped girls are?"

"Yes."

"How long have you known?"

"Hours."

"Was the information hard to come by?"

"Very."

"I see." Reverend Ebenezer's tone grew even more respectful. "But you did it. You found out."

"Yes. I did."

"This could be big, you know?"

"Bigger than big."

The reverend nodded in agreement. "When do we get them out?"

"The question is not when, but how."

"Knowing you, I imagine you have a plan."

Trina shook her head sadly. "That's why I called you." Pausing long enough to pin the blow-up exhibit on the wall, she frowned, her pretty face downcast. Gritting her teeth, she turned away, trying to hide her emotions. "This is where the girls are kept."

Reverend Ebenezer squinted in an effort to get a better look at the building in the photo. "That-that's the old Afro-American Cultural Center, isn't it?"

"Correct."

"But how---?"

"There is an underground area beneath the building. A long time ago before it was the cultural center, it was Little Rock AME Zion Church. The area beneath the church was a part of the Underground Railroad where slaves were hid. The church was built on top of it some time later."

Reverend Ebenezer felt this palms sweat. "But how do we get down there?"

"Trina shrugged. "Your guess is as good as mine, but if we are going to rescue the girls, we had better find out quick. Time is running out."

Reverend Ebenezer jumped up. "I will be in touch."

It was 10:00, Tuesday night. A fierce wind whipped through First Ward, howling furiously, sweeping 7th Street clean of soda cans and paper. It was dark and the rain was almost of biblical proportions. It poured.

For a long time nothing moved in the darkness until out of the deserted recesses of Myers Street, a figure emerged. Even though it was not cold, he flipped up the hood of his starter jacket while stuffing his hands into a pair of black latex gloves.

The rain and wind stung the face of the lone figure as he sliced through the night, and when he saw his shadow pop out from the under the flash of a streetlamp, he swung at it with a quick jab and a left hook.

At 10:10, the figure bounded up the steps of the abandoned Afro-American Cultural Center.

One...

Two...

Three...

Four.....

A few steps later he was on the top. Breathing abnormally, huffing hard, he tried to make it look as if he was seeking shelter from the storm because he knew he was being watched by someone....somewhere. Standing with his back to the door, the lone figure attached a small electronic eye just under the knob.

When he was finished, the lone figure ran around the corner where a blue Lincoln waited.

Trina kissed Geek on the cheek.

With the info gathered from the thermal imaging eye, Trina hoped that she and Reverend Ebenezer would be able to put together a good enough plan to save not only Shonda and the other girls, but herself as well. It was about to go down.

CHAPTER ELEVEN

Trina expected that question.

"Do you trust me?" Kofi inquired. When there was silence, he continued. "In Ghana, there is a saying: one does not drink medicine for a sick person. What that means is that if you are sick, you are the one that requires the remedy."

Trina wished that she had a little more leeway, but she knew she had to get on the inside as soon as possible if she was to rescue Shonda. That meant she had to play right into Kofi's plans.

"So, now I'm sick. If that's the best you can do—"

All throughout the night, Kofi had thought of his next move with Trina. By no means was he going to be able to rejoice about what he was about to do to her young life, but if he was to make it to the next level of his career, he had little choice. He refused to occupy the rest of his life with what could have been. This, he believed, was what he was born for and he burned to fulfill his potential. A lot was riding on his decision.

"Maybe I'm the one that's sick."

"Then, why don't you take your medicine?"

"This is serious, Trina. Really serious."

Trina stopped. She stared Kofi directly in his eyes. "As if I didn't know that."

"Wh-what do you mean?"

"All I know, Kofi, is that I'm in love with you. I tried not to let it happen, but no one has ever schooled me in the fine art of not doing what my heart is ordering me to do." Trina whispered softly. "This is not some pie-in-the-sky type love, Kofi. I honestly feel like it's the rest-of-my-life-in-progress." She smiled. "Is this the part where you tell me that we need to take some time off?"

"Not hardly, but there is something that you must know that only I can tell you."

Trina gripped Kofi's hand. "Then don't leave anything out except the part where you tell me that you don't feel as I do."

"How can a lie that big exist?"

"Any lie between two people who care about each other is too big."

Kofi looked away. "I wish to tell you about a conspiracy."

"I already know."

"You-you do?"

"Of course."

"Then what are we going to do?"

All of a sudden, the sunshine felt so warm to Kofi, and the world seemed ready to become a place of unspeakable joy, but still he had to play the hand he had been dealt. Or did he? As a compromise, he leaned over and kissed Trina on the cheek. He had made up his mind. He was going to reshuffle the deck and let the cards fall where they may.

The seconds ticked on.

Reverend Ebenezer texted Trina as Kofi walked her towards the edge of Freedom Park. The Charlotte police were getting the first reports of a missing, unidentified African girl from Ghana who had not come home from her part-time job. Around the same time, a couple in Northeast Charlotte discovered a note left by their daughter sitting on her computer. Earlier that same evening, Sheba Anthony had also not been accounted for.

Trina sighed. She could be next.

Strangely enough, within the space of seventy-two hours, the list of missing black girls had grown to almost a dozen. Even stranger was that they all had seemed to have vanished into thin air and no one suspected that the chain of missing girls was even remotely connected. *Yet.*

Trina knew what would happen next.

On the way to Kofi's car, Trina begged that nothing would go wrong. She realized that she would not be going home tonight.

When they reached the parking lot and Trina saw the long, black sedan driving slowly towards them, she took a long, deep breath. This was it.

What happened next took her by surprise.

Without warning, Kofi grabbed her by the arm and twisted her around. *"This way!"* he shouted. *"Let's go....Run!"*

On impulse, Kofi looked quickly over his shoulder as he and Trina ran away, out of the parking lot, in the direction of the main building, but no sooner had he dragged her up the hill behind Shelter # 2 than he saw them. Two men and a woman clustered around the entrance to the building, the alert look of the hunter etched on their faces. Kofi stiffened.

"They must have figured I was going to run."

"Who?!" Trina exclaimed, out of breath.

"Just be cool. We must find another way out of here. Where's another exit?"

Running along the concrete walkway, Kofi and Trina dashed around the pond, opposite the amphitheater. They moved by instinct rather than memory. Neither had entered or exited the park from this direction. All they knew was that they could no longer safely leave the way they had arrived. This rude awakening posed a big problem for them.

"This way!" Kofi shouted.

Feeling Trina close at his side, Kofi hoped they could outrun their pursuers. From behind them, they could hear a loud commotion.

"They're coming!" Trina shrieked. "They're after us!"

Glancing behind them, Kofi could clearly see the men and the woman scrambling down the hill. He gripped Trina's hands tighter, dragging her along the grassy knoll behind the restrooms. "This way. Let's go."

Stumbling across the grass, Trina could never recall running this fast and though she was breathing hard, her mind was moving even faster. She was determined to keep up.

Kofi turned left and after a few more steps, she realized that they weren't really putting that much distance between them and the people chasing them. She also noticed that she was sweating and that the bottoms of her feet tingled.

A little farther on, Trina felt as though someone was trying to rip her heart out of her chest, but she did see that they were pulling away, leaving their pursuers behind. Two steps later, she felt drugged, imprisoned inside a vacuum of inertia and for the first time didn't believe she couldn't lift her feet up one more time. It was then that Reverend Ebenezer pulled up.

"Hurry up," he commanded. "Get in.!"

The task force had been assembled. Reverend Ebenezer sat behind a desk in a makeshift office. This was Headquarters. FBI agents Bob Jacobs and Larry Hawkins were also present.

At the push of a button, the exterior door resounded with a metallic click, releasing the lock. Another FBI agent walked in. With him was Trina.

"Good Morning, Trina," Reverend Ebenezer said in greeting. He rose stiffly from behind the desk, extending his hand. "We have good news for you."

"You've rescued Shonda...the others."

"Yes, but first, the truth about Shonda." Reverend Ebenezer gazed at Trina. "Have a seat, please." He himself sat back down. "I think I need to explain a few things to you. To begin with, I am not a real reverend. I am a FBI agent. I have been on assignment here the last few years investigating The King and his organization."

Trina gasped in disbelief.

"Don't look so alarmed. "We found out quite some time ago that The King was moving his base of operations here and we needed a presence here if we were going to stop him."

"You mean—you mean that you are a fake?!"

The men in the room thought that was funny. Everyone, minus Trina, laughed.

"If it's any consolation too you, my name is really Ebenezer. You can still call me Reverend Ebenezer if you like." He grinned. "And while we're on the subject of what's fake and what's not......are you ready for this? Your friend Shonda was not a real student. She is a FBI agent. She was merely posing as a teenager."

"But I have been knowing Shonda for three years."

"That's just how good her cover was. Shonda is one of the best. Thanks to her and the info she was sending out from the location where she and the girls were, we were able to successfully bring them all out."

Almost immediate was the need to celebrate at the news of the rescue, but Trina was still too shocked at what she was hearing. "Thank God, it's over." Then her mood darkened. "I know that what Kofi did was wrong, but is there anything I can do to help him?" Trina paused. "After what he did, I know it may sound crazy, but I think he is a really good person."

"And you really, truly believe that?"

Trina nodded her head. "Yes, I do."

"Then why don't you tell him yourself." Reverend Ebenezer pushed a button on his desk and a second later, Kofi walked in. He was smiling. "Trina," Reverend Ebenezer said, "I'd like for you to meet FBI Agent Kofi Ebo."

BOOK THREE

CHAPTER TWELVE

Noon. The next day.

Trina pushed through the doors of the church hurriedly.

As she strolled down the empty interior of the church, she instantly experienced the almost uncontrollable urge to spin around and to run back out into the street. It was as if she was expected.

With a measure of pride, Reverend Ebenezer rushed from the study to greet her. He looked Trina in the eyes. "Today is the first day for the rest of your life." He pointed to a huge, glossy poster where those words were inscribed. "Today, you begin."

Trina already felt frightened, but didn't want to think about it. Yet she did because, for the most part, she didn't know what was happening although she knew it would happen today.

Throughout the whole ritual of making small talk, Trina had looked for distractions to help her counter how totally numb she felt, but, in a very short time, she had spiritually steamed up the muscles in her brain enough to get---whatever it was---out into the open.

"Well, what are you waiting on?" Reverend Ebenezer asked. "Go on and tell me what's on your mind."

"I had this dream last night."

Reverend Ebenezer smiled knowingly as he pointed to the sign again. "The dream was about your rebirth, your new life."

"But this is my life."

"Was. Past tense, Trina. This was your life." Reverend Ebenezer paced the floor. "Consider this. You are special. *Really special.*"

Trina was astonished at that remark. "How do you figure that?" she asked bluntly.

"Okay, here it is. You have been chosen to save teenagers from an early dietary graveyard." Reverend Ebenezer stared Trina in the eyes. "I know this is all strange and sudden, but it's all a part of what you must do to fulfill yourself."

"How do you know it's me?" When the reverend tried to walk away, Trina grabbed him by his arm. *"How do you know it's me?!"* she shrieked. "How do you know that I am the one?!" Trina struggled long enough with the temptation to voice her opinion that everyone may have been wrong about her. "How do you know that a mistake has not been made? Tell me," she screamed, "how do you know it's me!?"

Reverend Ebezener's face darkened. "There has not been a mistake." He glared at Trina. "You are the one so the only sensible thing for you to do is to believe."

Trina didn't know what to think.

"It's been quite a morning," Reverend Ebenezer chimed. "I must finish packing. My job is done here. I want you to go home."

Trina shook her head. "Not until I get some answers."

Reverend Ebenezer offered no protest. Instead, he wrote on a slip of church stationary. "Here, take this and go see the man whose name is written down."

"And then what?" When Reverend Ebenezer was silent, Trina whispered. "Answer me. And then what?"

"That is for you to find out."

As she stood at the doorway of her bedroom, she was surprised when she turned and saw her mother. The unexpected look of serenity on her mother's face caught her off-guard. She had never seem her look so calm before. "Your moment has come," Alfreda whispered. "Go."

"Go where?" Trina asked.

"To whatever awaits you."

Trina gritted her teeth and slowly turned away solemnly walking to the front door. Saying nothing, she raced into the oncoming traffic. It was as if her feet knew where to go.

Ten minutes later, the sky abruptly turned ugly as the mood of the morning became evil, like something out of a made-for-TV-movie. Trina gulped hard, trying to get the lump out of her throat.

She ran on.

After another mile or so as she crossed from one side of the street to the other, she shuddered as the sky darkened even more. It felt like the sky had eyes and that they were watching her. Trina fought back her fear.

She ran on.

After hearing a voice in her head, Trina calmed down, but before she was sure of what to do next, she found himself at her destination. She stopped in the church's parking lot and caught her breath.

"Go inside the church," the voice inside her head ordered.

Pausing just inside the church's door, Trina's body suddenly felt warm. She inhaled deeply and a strong whiff of incense tickled her nose. She found the fragrance appealing.

As she moved quietly through the silent sanctum, she numbly recognized how the church was a squeaky clean self-promotion of all the stuff in the Bible, and for a brief second, she stopped, standing mute in the eloquent dimness; not budging.

On the move again, her blood stirred. She crept forward more slowly now, almost on tip-toe until she reached the pastor's study where she yanked open the door without knocking.

"I am here," she said flatly. "*What now?*"

The preacher spoke calmly. "So you are."

Trina exhaled loudly. "Am I the one?"

"You do believe in the power of destiny, don't you?"

Trina remained silent.

"Well, don't you?!" the preacher boomed. He smirked. "Because if you need more time to think about it, then we have a big problem. Do you know why? The more you put off doing what you must do means that another child will eat another hamburger filled with pink slime. The fact that you are a coward will give food companies more time to entice another one of your peers into popping the top on another soda that will torture their kidneys." When Trina still refused to speak, the preacher's eyes widened. "This is not going to be easy, I see." He thumped Trina lightly in the chest with a cane. "You think you can fight the fire the fast food industry has started just by standing on the sidelines, blowing on the flames. Wake up, girl, your health is aflame and it's going to burn your life up. You must fight fire with fire" he chuckled.

"I only came for answers," Trina said softly, "not to fight anything or anyone."

The preacher acted as though Trina had never spoken. "It is essential that you keep in mind that we are on a timetable. Every minute you have must be put into this."

"But---"

The preacher continued to ignore Trina. "There is a clear reason why you do not understand the relationship between what you want to do and what fate has decided you must do. Soon," the old preacher warned, "you will learn."

"Learn what?"

Even though the old preacher found nothing suspicious about Trina's question, he slowly swaggered around to the other side of the study and grabbed a set of keys from a wooden rack. "Let's go," he ordered in a stern voice.

Driving fast, the old preacher ascended the mountain making Trina's ears pop as the pressure inside her head grew stronger.

Thirty minutes later when they entered a residential zone, the preacher sped past the pretty farms and pastures just inside the county line and took a crooked exit where they could, at once, spot the tops of a row of houses. Driving slower now, the preacher rode into a cluttered downtown district where the homes looked like they had been cut out of a magazine with a giant pair of scissors.

The car stopped in front of a house with a gabled, green roof.

When the preacher knocked on the door, Trina heard a thudding boom as if whoever was on the other side of the closed door had fallen out of a chair, crashing onto the floor, but when they stepped inside, she saw nothing that would have made the thundering noise.

In a voice that sounded caked with gravel, a second preacher croaked. "Have a seat."

If there had ever been a time in her life when she felt dwarfed by another human being, Trina knew this was it. This preacher, though pudgy and round, reeked with power. Trina had no idea where the notion had come from, but suddenly she experienced the very real sensation that the man had been waiting on her for quite some time and he displayed his impatience with her by rolling his eyes and drumming his beefy fingers on his desk.

"By God, chile," he snapped, "do you know what time it is!?"

Trina shook his head.

"Just today, a study came out that declared that junk food was as addictive as cocaine and cigarettes. And if that isn't enough, one in every three children is overweight. Junk food has single-handedly transformed your generation into the first one in the history of this land that may have a shorter life-span than their parents." The preacher was clearly upset. "Your generation is a group of teenaged scavengers who say ugly things out of your mouths and who put even worse things into your mouths."

"I'm sorry," Trina whimpered. "Wh-who are you? What is your name?"

"I have no name." The vacant expression on the preacher's face deepened, "but I am the one who has the task of preparing you for the journey that lies ahead of you."

CHAPTER FOURTEEN

On the surface, Trina gave the illusion that she was cool and in control, but the truth was that she was scared of the preacher, but far more frightening was what would await her once the old man sent her on her journey.

Without any tenderness in his coarse voice, the preacher spoke in a tone so cold that Trina wondered if he possessed any emotions.

"Nothing will be withheld from you," the Wizard announced before turning away, pretending he was not concerned. Chuckling to show he didn't resent her presence, the preacher plopped down in a chair. "Teens have considerable enemies, so yes, it has been difficult for me to watch helplessly as you have conducted herself so foolishly, wanting to be a beauty queen. But you have come as I always knew you would. That is what matters. Nothing else." Apparently aware of Trina's thoughts, the preacher grinned, showing stained, cracked teeth. "Today, you get answers." He stood tall, now speaking in a celebratory tone. "Today, you will begin your Shero's journey and today will mark the start of this country's redemption from unhealthy food choices." The preacher thrust a glass into Trina's trembling hand. "Here, drink this libation."

Feeling a chill run up her spine, Trina grasped the golden goblet and raised it to her chocolate cheeks. She tightly closed her eyes while she consumed the contents.

"At last!" the preacher shrieked wildly. "At long last!" He happily slapped Trina on the back. "At long last, the shoe is on the other foot."

All at once, Trina felt a pleasant tingling inside her body, but a second later, her body shook so hard her bones rattled uncontrollably. It stopped and soon she was able to resume breathing properly, but with this return to normalcy, she understood that she had undergone an enormous change. She felt somehow cheated. *She had come for confirmation---not transformation!*

For a full five minutes, the preacher allowed Trina to pace the floor in silent contemplation, then commanded that she stand still. *"It is time!"*

Strangely, Trina wasn't expecting anything else, but before she could react, the preacher was forcibly waving a ceremonial mask in her face. The man was now alive with power.

"Behold!" he yelled.

Trina tried to pretend that she wasn't afraid, but the leather mask did frighten her somewhat and she felt the fear mounting in her chest as she observed the preacher fingering the mask as if it was a live pet.

"You must lose all fear of the mask," the preacher commanded. "The mask cannot harm you. Are you ready to see?"

"I-I'm ready."

"No. No, you're not," the preacher countered sharply. "I can still hear the fear in your voice. Release your inner fears and the mask will become your protector, another part of you."

The preacher's tone became tender and dreamy, coming from afar. "Are you now ready?"

Trina took a deep breath. "Yes, I am ready."

With his stubby fingers intertwined in the gaping eye holes of the mask, the preacher leaned forward and carefully unhooked the twin, gold clasps on the back of the mask and when he had spread it at its base, the mask appeared to yawn. Then slowly, he extended it forward, towards Trina's face. "The mask will open your eyes and heart."

Trina inhaled.

Going over her head, the mask smelled like it had been scented with Lemon Pledge. Gulping air, she overcame the first wave of fear, but when the mask settled full over her face, the emotional impact was so explosive, she wanted to yank the leather contraption from her face and fling it to the floor.

"Breathe.....Slowly. Your fear will recede." The preacher made the announcement like a movie director conducting auditions. "Look me in my eyes."

For Trina, trying to maintain eye contact was extremely hard because the peep holes in the mask restricted her vision. Even worse was her breathing. Her nose felt packed with cotton and the hole designed for her mouth was so extraordinarily constricting, she wasn't sure if she could utter words. Generally speaking, she felt vulnerable and powerless, a feeling that slowly engulfed her.

"Now, close your eyes."

Trina didn't expect this!

The vision was a drama of past, present, and future. Trina felt both scared and excited by the mask and its aura, its mystery.....its possibilities.

She gazed out of the eyes of the mask, but didn't see what she thought she would see. She smiled at the vision because it soothed her, but in the vision, she kept noticing things. *The quaint, little street where she had* lived as a child was quite hectic for this time of night. As her father stepped out of the house into the front yard, Trina gawked at all the men and women who were lined up outside, trying to look natural.

Her father grunted. There were no words, but after a few awkward moments of silence, he spoke. "To me, this day, has been born a child."

At the announcement, the sky above their house was lit up with a brilliant blast of red-hot lightning that opened up a kaleidoscopic panorama from which thunder boomed down like a big African drum.

"Bring the child forth." It was the wizard, much younger then, who spoke.

The neighborhood women danced in jubilation when they laid eyes on the tiny child. The men, for some unknown reason, tore through the streets in a solemn rush. Trina followed them with her eyes as they navigated their way past a rock-strewn path until it angled to the left behind an old gnarled tree that rested next to a shallow bed of dead grass.

With effortless agility, the men accelerated into the dark, not slowing until they had arrived at the ceremonial hut at the fringes of the neighborhood.

"The child has come!" they shouted gleefully. "The child has come!"

Trina, breathing hard behind the mask, watched in fascination as her father placed the child in a crude, iron crib which sat in the center of the hut, surrounded by a circle of burning, long-stemmed candles. Another circle of candles blazed hotly outside the diameter, forming a fiery aisle of flames. All the men, except the bare-chested wizard, exited the inner circle, disappearing into the darkness of the ceremonial hut. The powerfully-built wizard stooped low over the infant, drawing heavily from a fat, gourd pipe. He blew short bursts of thick, green smoke over the four corners of the wrought-iron baby crib and then waved his muscular hands violently through the hovering clouds of smoke, dissipating them into eternity. He then stood upright and chanted loudly. Next, he pulled the covers from the baby's face. Trina was astonished. She was the infant!

The men, led by her father, catapulted out of the nothingness into the flickering brilliance of the burning candles. The men---all of them---danced into the arc of the flames, their bare feet pounding intensely against the mud-baked floor. These were strong, virile urban warriors. On they danced, their black bodies swaying in unison, flowing timelessly, but her father leaped higher, bent deeper, and whirled more precisely than any of the others as he led them through the fire.

Trina looked on, transfixed.

The wizard trumpeted the good news to the heavens and beyond. "The child is come."

The mask oozed with sweat. Trina snatched it off.

Trina had lost all concept of time so she had no idea if it was day or night. All she knew was that she was off the mountain and was now standing in the study at Reverend Ebenezer's house, staring vacantly at the golden scroll she had been handed.

"What was his name?"

The reverend scowled at Trina. "His name is not important. Besides, if he had wanted to let you know what his name was, he would probably have told you before he carried you up the mountain-top to see yourself. What is important is that you study what is written on that scroll." The reverend left.

Nothing was normal now, and no one was what they appeared to be. Trina giggled. The wizard with no name who was now a preacher. The reverend who was a FBI agent who was now her mentor in whatever came next in this bizarre journey. Sometimes, she wondered if her mother and father were who they said they were. Trina giggled some more.

Taking a seat, she inspected the outside of the tightly-rolled scroll, then slit the silk cord that secured it. With a hiss, the paper rolled itself out like a cat's tongue. Trina didn't know what was happening, but instantly, without reading, she knew what the document contained. It was like someone had split her brain open, poured in the info, and then fused her head shut. How eerie. Struggling, but determined to control her nerves, she let the new knowledge wash over her like rain, but the moment she felt relaxed, Reverend Ebenezer was at her side.

"I know," Trina whispered. "My education is complete."

The reverend laughed coolly. "It has just begun."

"It's like all the knowledge I didn't need has been squeezed out of my head." Trina paused. "This new knowledge is almost too much to bear."

"It's more than mere knowledge, my friend. It's magic"

Staring out of the window with its bright yellow curtains, Trina saw the moon as it slowly slid across the horizon like a spool of creamy, golden butter. She could not rest.

"The magic of knowledge is meant to make one uncomfortable." Reverend Ebenezer smiled. "What bothers you most, the fact that you are a messenger, or the fact that you are not going to be a beauty queen?" When it took Trina longer to respond that usual, Reverend Ebenezer sighed. "Go home, my child. As fate would have it, there is one who will seek to destroy you."

"Who is he?"

"You will know when you know." This time the reverend exited the room quickly. They would meet again soon.

It was two in the morning when Trina finally arose from bed. She couldn't sleep. For the longest time, she had been bothered by the morbid thought of someone wanting to destroy her.

The King. That's who it was.

For the tiniest of seconds, with her small dainty fists balled up, she stood still. This gesture made her feel like a fighter, a true warrior queen. If it was war the food industry wanted, she would fight fire with fire.

Then on impulse, she marched into the bathroom and shaved off all her hair!

She was surprised at how powerful she felt. It was almost as if a hidden reserve of strength had been buried under her hair. She felt like growling as she deliberately basked in the sheer rapture of the stark, raw energy that sparkled through her body.

To her amazement, she loved her bald, new look. Too her it represented the moment of truth where beauty and brains met to form a complete whole. She would never be the same again. Ever.

CHAPTER FIFTEEN

It was on!

The first issue on her agenda now that she had accepted her commission was how best to add some bite to her new position. After all, she had no skills to speak of. That could turn out to be a big problem for her despite all the assurances she had gotten from Reverend Ebenezer and her family. In the back of her mind, she did hope that they knew what they were talking about or else she could be in a lot of trouble if she ever had a face-to-face encounter with The King. She was convinced that he had a few good tricks up his sleeve.

After thinking of all the movies she had seen where the good guys got the worse of the fight, she started to sweat. Being a rookie in a battle with an all-around veteran bad guy was more than a minor glitch. In reality, it could result in a major meltdown for her. Putting on her best game face, she still understood that she would be dead in her tracks if she didn't do something immediately to boost her chances of success. She could barely hide her anxiety because the one thing she knew to be true was that there was a direct link between having no power and losing. If what everyone said was true, then what played a key role in a dogfight was not the bark of the dog but his bite.

"So be it!" Trina shouted at the heavens. *"So be it!"*

Nothing earth-shattering or life-altering happened. In a funny sort of way, she wasn't surprised, but just the same, she uttered the words once more. **_"So be it!"_** Still......nothing. Suddenly, Trina felt like she was in big trouble.

In her head, Trina went over her game plan. Now that she had pinpointed the identity of her enemy, she felt the only legitimate way to beat him would be to work her way up the ranks. That's the way boxers did it. They didn't just run out and jump into the ring with the champion no matter how good they thought they were. Instead, they had a few tune-up fights to prepare them for their one shot at superstardom. She saw no reason why that approach wouldn't work for her. Anything was worth a try. No true fan of combat would hold it against her if she tested herself against a few scrub restaurants to hone her skills before she took on the giants of the food industry.

But where would she find her first fight? She chuckled. Maybe she should post on FaceBook. If that didn't work, as she was certain it wouldn't, maybe she could dig up something from who knows where. And while she was thinking about it, she knew it would probably be equally as hard to find a clue on either

Instagram or Pinterest that would ultimately lead her to the identity of a diner she could beat up on.

The more she thought about, the more it seemed like a conspiracy. Why else would she ordered to take a leave of absence from her summer vacation to save the world, and then not give her proper instructions on how to perform her duties. Where was her crystal ball? Did she have to round up her own helpers? At least, she had Geek. Finally, something she could feel good about. Geek. Trina felt relieved.

Then something else dawned on her. Despite all the evidence to the contrary, she knew that she would somehow receive all the training required to kick butt.

Trina dreamed a dream that night.

Though the dream was brief, it was not funny. She had just closed her eyes two minutes past the hour and though she didn't like being machine-gunned with a cast of characters that made her uncomfortable, she couldn't afford to wake up until she had some clue as to why they were disturbing the peace of her sleep.

Without warning, she interrupted the characters.

Four of the characters seated around the table, including SpongeBob Squarepants and Dora the Explorer, were cartoon figures. The other remaining figure was her.

SpongeBob Squarepants made a muscle. He wanted Trina to see that he was a lot stronger than people gave him credit for. Dora pointed out how good she was at finding stuff.

The meeting was supposed to have been with a group of talented wizards who had come to brainstorm about her current mission. They were scheduled to conjure up all the ancient knowledge, wisdom, and understanding of the ancestors so she could use it in her fight.

Instead, each of the present participants, SpongeBob Squarepants in particular, wanted to take part in her Shero's journey.

At 2:15 am, Trina's voice broke through the din as the cartoon characters argued with each other. "Need I remind each of you that no matter how loud you get that none of you is going to accompany me. And SpongeBob, if I were you, I would go on back to Bikini Bottom and save it. Let me save Teen-age America, okay?"

The cartoon characters were unfazed.
At seven o'clock in the morning, Trina realized that she faced an emergency.

CHAPTER SIXTEEN

Until now, her life had been composed of a series of baby steps and bunny hops, hardly the moves needed to kick-off her career as a Shero, and the fuzzy picture she had of herself as one didn't help much either. Often, it made her laugh. This time, she made a face. She guessed she would spend the next few years learning her craft at the knees of a group of enlightened teachers. She also guessed these would be her "missing years". Every great deliverer had them. Even Jesus had those years which couldn't be accounted for. Most scholars believe those three years were spent secretly studying with the Essenes, a group who schooled him in the knowledge he would need to compete with a world that had never seen the likes of someone quite like him before.

Now, it was her turn.

Trina suddenly felt like she had been beamed up into another life where she had reached another level of her existence, but when were her teachers going to appear. All she had been told was that when she was ready, her teachers would appear. She laughed. It couldn't have been any more mysterious than that. Guessing again, she imagined she would lose a lot of sleep before this was all over with.

Then, for the very first time, it abruptly became clear what her mission and message were. She ran to find her father.

"So, now you see."

"Yes, my father, my eyes have been opened."

"I'm proud of you, my child."

Trina paused, letting her head clear because she recognized that she was up against a very formidable foe. Sensing her disadvantages, she felt a cold chill run up her spine. She prayed that she would find gaps and weaknesses in her enemy. She would appreciate that very much.

In a flash, she mentally examined the roots of her enemy's existence, picking away at the layers as if they were the crust of a flaky apple pie, but every time a pattern began to take shape, it would just as quickly disappear. This was due to her enemy's amazing ability to hide, to run in and out of everyone's life with such ease. Now, this was real magic. How could she defend against such incredible power?

"I know you are probably wondering what a fine mess you have gotten yourself into, but this is for real. This is no designer revolution." Trina's father shook with outrage. "Fast food joints have brought us so much grief, and now stand ready to unleash a new wave of dietary woes upon us if you don't stop them."

"But this will be a fight like never before."

"But one that must be fought just the same."

"That's the scary part," Trina admitted openly, "but what must be must be. Still, I just wish people would just say no to Ronald McDonald. That sure would make my job easier."

Trina's father didn't seem to like her last comment. "What you don't seem to understand yet, Princess, is that being forearmed with knowledge is necessary to success." His expression did not change although his tone did soften somewhat. "Pay attention to what comes next to you. What may seem like a wild goose chase won't be, and though you may not understand, all will be revealed." He dropped his head. "Your time has come. Go, find yourself, Princess."

Trina did not know where she was going, but she was being tugged along by a momentum she couldn't fight or resist. She condemned herself for not turning around and running, but how could she flee from destiny...from herself...from The Book of Life? Whatever awaited her, she believed, would represent the end of the world as she knew it. This was do-or-die, an ordeal compounded by the fact that she had no idea what was on the other end of the stick. Yet she was committed to find out. She had to know.

There were so many moments when Trina felt like she was out of her league. In the beginning, all she had wanted to do was to be a beauty queen. Now, it seemed like she was out trying to earn her caped crusader license. Still, she knew she had to see how this would all play out. She had to find out what would happen once she had turned the page, having closed this chapter of her life. This morning, if nothing else was certain, it felt like, for once, she was living on borrowed time.

New beginnings could be scary.

From out of nowhere, a light rain had started to fall on the city and even at a little before ten o'clock in the morning, traffic swirled by like a viper's nest of swarming cars. She watched from the safety of the sidewalk as buses, trucks and cars whizzed by. Then she got a hunch. Something had happened up the block.

She walked faster.

Within minutes, she was standing at the fringes of a heavily-cordoned off area, enclosed with the standard yellow police ribbon. Uniformed and plainclothes cops stood around the crime scene, whispering and making gestures. The atmosphere was tense.

Trina watched as a big police officer bullied his way through the crowd until he reached the front of the crime scene. There he issued commands and orders to everyone. He received hostile stares from the gathering crowd who soon began shouting angrily.

"Sir" someone asked loudly. "How did this happen?"

"Clear out of here," the big policeman roared in reply. "Go home."

"What do you intend to do about this now that it has happened?"

Trina moved closer. "What's going on?" she wanted to know.

Even though she did not know what had happened, she found it hard not to identify with the angry crowd who seemed ready to riot at any given second.

"Go home," the big cop thundered, "and watch it on the news or I will have all of you arrested."

Trina made a mental note to herself not to move a muscle.

"*Murder! Murder!*" the crowd chanted.

When the coroner pulled up to pronounced the death of the victim, Trina saw the body of the victim. It was an old, black man.

"*Murder!*" she shouted along with all the others. "*Murder!*"

It started to rain harder and just as the police started to move in with their riot gear, Reverend Ebenezer was at Trina's side, tugging her away from the mob and pushing her into a waiting car.

"Let's go," he instructed her firmly. "Your job here is done."

On the one occasion when she had wanted to stand her ground, Trina was forced into the car and without any delay, the vehicle sped into the oncoming traffic.

Reverend Ebenezer hugged Trina delightfully. "Do you know what you just witnessed?"

"Of course," Trina replied sadly, "the murder of another human being."

"Or so it seemed."

"B-But----"

"Have you forgotten what you were told about nothing being what it appeared to be?"

Trina remembered.

"What appeared to you as the lifeless body of an old man was merely the destruction and death of American civilization by the fork and spoon. In theory, the old man represented the potential power and strength of America to feed itself with wholesome food, but since the country has failed to do so, the old man was symbolic of the 580,000 deaths annually that are caused by unhealthy eating practices and inactivity."

The news shocked Trina.

"For decades, we have been taught that cigarette smoking was the culprit, but food is even more dangerous. 580,000 deaths," Reverend Ebenezer proclaimed. "That's twenty times more deadly than drug use, and thirteen times greater than the death toll caused by guns." He cleared his throat. "This country was founded upon the agricultural knowledge that it could produce food and feed itself, but somewhere along the way, greed grew up quicker than any crop. Modern day America was built primarily on the harvest of that greed."

"So just like the robber barons of the times wanted to monopolize the railroads and oil wells-----"

"Not monopolize," the reverend corrected, "but control. Consider this, Trina. All the great wealth gatherers of those days were all taught that greed was good and that money was king. The 'profits before people' rule of law had its origin there."

"Wow!"

"But that's just the tip of the iceberg. Among these prophets of profit was the father of the fast food nation." The reverend was almost finished. "That is enough for now," he whispered.

"But who was the murderer of that old man?"

"Ignorance."

Trina was confused. "But how do I use magic against myth?"

"You will soon know."

CHAPTER SEVENTEEN

Later that same evening, Trina felt like the joke was on her, but she was beginning to get the picture. She was almost embarrassed, but it was nothing to be ashamed of or to laugh at. Most people had this phony concept of magic as something from the pages of Harry Potter when the greatest magic of all was knowledge. The Wizard of Oz, or no other wizard for that matter, possessed the power to explain away myth or to exorcise ignorance. Only true wisdom and knowledge was that powerful a force.

Once she was dressed and had eaten, she again experienced the need to learn something. Ultimately, she ended up at the Center of Hope, a homeless shelter for women on Spratt Street. Upon her arrival, she saw that a television crew was there.

"How many more are there?" someone asked.

"How do I know?" a representative from the shelter barked. "One is too many."

Trina figured they were talking about the women who were in the shelter.

"I don't understand any of this," the news reporter remarked.

Trina didn't either, but she watched as black women wandered aimlessly about the premises as if in search of something or someone. Trina wanted to know what it was that had been lost. The women searched here...there...everywhere. Still, they came up empty, finding nothing.

After several more minutes of hunting, Trina could see that the women's spirit seemed to be crushed as they each appeared to be suffocating from their horrible loss----whatever it was. Trina became obsessed with the women and their "treasure hunt" as she wondered what loss could cause so much pain.

"You'll never guess."

Reverend Ebenezer's voice startled Trina.

She jumped back, then recovered upon realizing who her companion was. "What are they looking for?"

"First of all, they are not homeless. They're soulless." Reverend Ebenezer closed his eyes, standing stiff." What they have lost is their self-esteem and this loss has reached epidemic proportions among black women everywhere. Without self-esteem, women cannot succeed. A lifetime of unhealthy eating habits has literally enslaved tens of thousands of women within the prisons of their own inferiority."

"How did they get this way?"

A faraway look glazed Reverend Ebenezer's eyes. "It starts when they are children, with their first Happy Meal."

"How?"

"When children began to associate food with fun and toys, they lose their capacity to appreciate the true value of food. At that point, food becomes a sort of entertainment for them, and they spend the rest of their lives chasing down colorful boxes of fun to fix meals with. Their hunt from then on is for foods that nourish their imagination rather than for food that nourish their bodies." Reverend Ebenezer chuckled. "Two billion dollars a year is spent by food companies to entice kids with their products, and once they hook them, they are loyal for life. Theses soulless women are the by-products of those products."

But what can I do?"

"You must rescue them."

"How?" Trina smiled sadly. "What magic is there for such a sad situation?"

"The magic of good nutrition," Reverend Ebenezer responded coolly. "Women who have not been taught how to eat healthy compete with one another in seeing who can withstand the most injury from their improper diet. A diet high in sugar, salt, and saturated fats are the major causes of four of the six leading causes of death in this country. Diabetes, brought on by bad food, is a major cause of blindness and amputation while bone loss is caused by osteoporosis. Unknown to women is the truth that proper eating gives birth to power which is the magic bullet that humans have sought and fought over since the dawn of time. Do you understand, my child?"

Trina nodded her head. "Women suffer because we lack the power of eating right. Is that it?"

"Close. Power is the yardstick by which everything else is measured, but self-esteem is the litmus test for how much power a person, man or woman, can acquire."

"Why is that?"

"Because of this universal truth: _you only get what you deserve_." Reverend Ebenezer grasped Trina's hand. "You must feel as if you deserve it in order for you to get it. You must make demands. You must demand that life award you. Life is not a banquet for beggars. It is a feast for the wise. Remember that, Trina."

Trina promised that she would never forget that lesson.

"Keeping that in mind, you can contribute a lot by raising the dietary consciousness of the teen-ager world, but change cannot come without awareness."

Trina took a deep breath. "I think I would rather fight dragons and evil wizards than to fight against---"

"The worldwide epidemic of poor nutrition. You must use the magic of organization and unity to address and to attack the problem."

Trina's head began to pound. "I-I can't do this. It is too much. I don't want to be the chosen one any more."

Reverend Ebenezer shook his head. "It is too late for tears now, Trina. We all have a cross to bear. This one is yours."

"But why?"

"Who knows why. All I know is that Teen-age America needs you. Do you understand, Trina?"

"Yes, I understand, but that doesn't make it any easier."

Carefully observing the expression on Trina's face, Reverend Ebenezer sighed loudly. "We all know what happens when things fall apart, but what about when people believe that things work that don't."

"Now, you're confusing me." Trina was honest.

"Have you ever been in a building with an elevator. What's the first thing you do once you step inside. You hit the close door button. Sure, the door closes, but not because you pressed the button. Do you know why?"

Trina shook her head.

"The button is what is called a dummy button. It's called that because it doesn't work. The button was placed there to give you the illusion of control, but it is totally useless. We think it works so we press it. That's a powerful trick and who doesn't love magic." Reverend Ebenezer grinned. "Ever been standing on the street corner at a light that took too long to change. Most people would push the button at the crosswalk to speed up the process."

"I've done that," Trina admitted.

"Well, you wasted your time."

Trina covered her face with her hands. "Another dummy button?"

"Yes. The lights are regulated by automatic timers, so no matter how often you press the button, it won't have any effect, but doesn't it feel good to believe that you have control. It's the placebo effect. Look that up if you don't know what it is."

"It's where you give a person with a headache a sugar pill instead of a real pain pill. The headache goes away because the person thought he was taking something to relieve the pain when in actuality, he wasn't."

"Precisely." Reverend Ebenezer sounded pleased. "Which can only mean one thing. People have the power to change the conditions of their lives. They only need a reason to believe they can. No matter how desperate the situation, people who believe they can, can triumph and prevail." He wrapped his arms around Trina's shoulder. "Let me give you one more example, then explain the solution. You ready?"

Trina shrugged. "I guess."

"In the winter, you can go into any big company and look at the walls. One thing you are sure to see is a heat thermostat. And what company doesn't want to keep its workers warm when it is freezing outside? But guess what? Those thermostats don't work. The controls don't do anything."

"Another dummy?"

"Think about it. Companies are not just going to let workers run up their electric bill by turning up the heat whenever they feel like it, so they do what, Trina?"

"Give them magic, the illusion of control."

"It's the greatest show on earth," Reverend Ebenezer smiled, "but get this. Even though the dummy control doesn't turn up the heat, the cold worker believes in it. Guess what happens?"

"The worker warms up?"

"Right again." Reverend Ebenezer gave Trina a playful squeeze. "Powerful stuff, this placebo effect. Real magic."

A light popped on in Trina's head. She smiled. "I get it. I'm not a Messiah or a Deliverer, am I? I'm a placebo."

Reverend Ebenezer nodded in agreement. "People need to be able to see a visible figment of their dreams and goals. In the case of the cold worker, we already know that the thermostat doesn't work, yet the worker feels warm. He's doing it, but he doesn't have enough belief in himself to reach the conclusion that he can do for himself so the thermostat represents only a physical extension of his own inner magic. People need to believe, but they view themselves in such a powerless way that they believe they need a Messiah."

Upon hearing this, Trina's shoulders slumped.

Reverend Ebenezer embraced her tighter. "I know," he winked knowingly, "just when you were staring to get into the idea of being a magician or a wizard, here comes the truth. But keep in mind that you don't need magic to introduce a person to the magic in themselves. You just need to show them how much you believe in yourself."

"It's just that I feel like I'm a trickster."

"Listen, my friend, it's either us or them."

"Them?"

"The bad guys. There is a saying: 'What luck it is for rulers that men do not think'. What does that mean to you?"

"If people thought for themselves, there would be no need for rulers. Right?"

Another nod from the reverend. "It's the ones like you who must counter the ones who will use the placebo effect to keep the people in bondage. You must free them."

Trina sighed. "I guess I can get used to being a human thermostat control." She laughed. "Or a dummy stop light control button."

"I don't see that."

"You-you don't?"

Reverend Ebenezer laughed. "I see you more as a sugar pill."

Spinning around on her toes like a ballet dancer, Trina laughed happily. "One sugar pill dipped in chocolate coming up!" She shook her head. "I would have never guessed that this was what was on the other end of the stick."

"Long live wellness" Reverend Ebenezer chanted.

"Long live good health," Trina chimed in.

COMING SOON

THE LAST SUPPER